I CAN LEARN

A HANDBOOK FOR PARENTS, TEACHERS, AND STUDENTS

Prepared by the
Special Education Division

Publishing Information

I Can Learn: A Handbook for Parents, Teachers, and Students was authorized by Assembly Bill 3040, Chapter 1501, Statutes of 1990, and prepared under contract number 8335 between the Special Education Division, California Department of Education, and the San Jose State University Foundation. The manuscript was reviewed by the Special Education Division and edited in the Publications Division by Janet Lundin. This publication was designed and prepared for photo-offset production by the staff of the Publications Division, with the cover and interior design created by Juan Sanchez. Typesetting was done by Carey Johnson.

This document was published by the California Department of Education, 721 Capitol Mall, Sacramento, California (mailing address: P.O. Box 944272, Sacramento, CA 94244-2720). It was printed by the Office of State Printing and distributed under the provisions of the Library Distribution Act and *Government Code* Section 11096.

ISBN 0-8011-1140-4

Ordering Information

Copies of this publication are available for $8.50 each, plus shipping and handling charges. California residents are charged sales tax. Orders may be sent to the Publications Division, Sales Office, California Department of Education, P.O. Box 271, Sacramento, CA 95812-0271; FAX (916) 323-0823. See the inside back cover for complete information on payment, including credit card purchases. Prices on all publications are subject to change.

A partial list of other educational resources available from the Department also appears on the inside back cover. In addition, an illustrated *Educational Resources Catalog* describing publications, videos, and other instructional media available from the Department can be obtained without charge by writing to the address given above or by calling the Sales Officeat (916) 445-1260.

Notice

The guidance in *I Can Learn* is not binding on local educational agencies or other entities. Except for the statutes, regulations, and court decisions that are referenced herein, *I Can Learn* is exemplary, and compliance with it is not mandatory. (See *Education Code* Section 33308.5.)

Prepared for publication
by CSEA members.

Contents

*Chapter III was added after the project had been completed.

Part Two: Gathering the Team—Finding Solutions

Preface

All children are special, and all children can learn. That is the premise of *I Can Learn*. It is our hope that this book will serve as a tool to help parents and teachers in the important work of helping children with special needs to be full participants in our society.

This is the third printing of *I Can Learn*. In it, the authors share their experiences in teaching students so that others can benefit from these ideas in their classrooms and homes. We believe the partnership of teacher and parent is a major factor in students' success.

The California Department of Education was authorized by Assembly Bill 3040 in 1990 to develop guidelines for teaching students with learning disabilities. As a result, the Department has developed program content that applies to any student experiencing a problem in learning and that emphasizes the role of the classroom teacher and the parent in creating an environment in which all students can succeed.

We want to thank the parents and educators who contributed to the publication of these guidelines. We trust that *I Can Learn* will continue to be a valuable resource to be shared among teachers, parents, and students so all children can learn.

DELAINE EASTIN
State Superintendent of Public Instruction

DHYAN LAL
Deputy Superintendent
Specialized Programs Branch

LEO D. SANDOVAL
Assistant Superintendent and Director
Special Education Division

Acknowledgments

This publication was developed through a contract with the San Jose State University Foundation. Mary Male was the Contract Director, and Janny Latno-Yamate was the Project Director. The work was conducted by a development team assisted by an advisory committee representing a broad spectrum of individuals, organizations, and public agencies involved in the education of students experiencing learning difficulties in school.

This publication was made possible through the efforts and legislation authored by Assemblywoman Jackie Speier, who has demonstrated her commitment to children with learning difficulties.

The titles and organizations of persons listed in this section were current when this publication was developed.

Development Team

Barbara Bryant Nolan, Author/Consultant; Director of Special Education, Orinda Union Elementary School District

Christopher Harris, Author/Consultant; Director, Chartwell School, Seaside

Janny Latno-Yamate, Project Director; Resource Specialist, Vallejo City Unified School District

Michael Spagna, Author/Consultant; Professor, Department of Special Education, California State University, Northridge

Susan Westaby, Consultant, Special Education Division, California Department of Education, Sacramento

William Wilson, Author/Consultant; Professor and Chair, Department of Special Education, San Francisco State University

Jeff Zettel, Consultant, Curriculum, Instruction, and Assessment Division, California Department of Education, Sacramento

Advisory Committee

Diana Berliner, Resource Specialist, Eureka High School

Kay Bodinger, Special Education Parent Facilitator Program, San Diego City Unified School District

Jeff Braden, Professor, Department of Educational Psychology, University of Wisonsin, Madison

Carol Brunett, Program Specialist, Greater Anaheim SELPA

Nancy Cushen White, Learning Specialist, San Francisco Unified School District and the University of California, San Francisco

Lou Denti, Program Director, Learning Handicapped Program, Division of Special Education and Rehabilitation Services, San Jose State University

Joan Esposito, Executive Director, Dyslexia Awareness and Resource Center, Santa Barbara

Nancy Flynn, Director of Special Education, Tracy Elementary School District and Tracy Joint Union High School District

Len Garfinkel, Graduate Student, San Francisco State University

Michael Goodman, School Psychologist, Gilroy Unified School District

Dan Graham, Principal, College Park Elementary School, Irvine Unified School District

Frank Graham-Caso, Teacher, San Diego City Unified School District

Gloria Heinemann, Acting Director of Special Education, Tracy Elementary School District and Tracy Joint Union High School District

Rob Kelley, Software Applications Specialist, Hewlett-Packard Company, Palo Alto

Bob and Yana Livesay, Directors, Dyslexia Treatment and Counseling Center, San Jose

Mary Male, Professor, Division of Special Education and Rehabilitation Services, San Jose State University

Shannon O'Hara, Teacher, Mt. Diablo Unified School District, Pleasant Hill

John Sanchez, Teacher, Covina-Valley Unified School District

Gary Seaton, Director, SELPA, San Luis Obispo County Office of Education

Jim Simonds, School Psychologist, Yucaipa-Calimesa Joint Unified School District

Kay Stanton, Special Education Coordinator, Glenn County Office of Education, Willows

Jim Swanson, Director, Child Development Center, University of California, Irvine

Elise Thurau, Legislative Assistant to Assemblywoman Jackie Speier, California State Assembly, Sacramento

Robert Verhoogen, Pediatrician, California Pacific Medical Center, San Francisco

Yana Livesay and Larry W. Douglass provided additional material to the Special Education Division.

Introduction

$\mathbf{T}$his document responds to the Legislature's intent to develop guidelines for specific learning disabilities and related disorders as enacted in Assembly Bill 3040 (1990) and Assembly Bill 2773 (1992). AB 3040 deals with specific learning disabilities. AB 2773 deals with dyslexia, attention deficit disorder (ADD), and attention deficit hyperactivity disorder (ADHD). These terms are defined in the Glossary.

This document differs from the typical special education program guidelines published by the California Department of Education. Rather than setting forth guidelines for the operation and administration of programs, it is a resource book for teachers and parents. The content emphasizes timely intervention in the general education classroom to prevent students, their parents, and teachers from becoming frustrated. Students can receive help before they fail in school or are referred for assessment for special education programs. In addition, information is included about how to structure school programs so that *all* students can succeed. As much as possible the document is written in ordinary language. To help readers, a glossary of technical terms appears in the last section of this publication.

In addition to providing information about the background of *I Can Learn,* this introduction contains some basic assumptions for providing instruction, the purpose of this publication, approaches to children's problems with learning and performance, content and organization of this publication, uses for the information in this publication, benefits of using the information, limitations of this publication, and answers to commonly asked questions.

Basic Assumptions

The material presented in this document is based on the following four assumptions:

1. All children want to learn.
2. Most misbehavior or poor academic performance is neither willful nor malicious.
3. Teachers want to teach effectively.
4. All parents want to understand and support their child's learning.

In addition, the following are current concepts regarding the provision of instruction:

- There is probably no one general reading or instructional program that meets the needs of all students in a class.
- Some students will require direct instruction in the basic skills of reading, writing, and spelling in order to learn those skills.

- Early identification of a learning problem is essential so that intervention can reduce school failure and the loss of self-esteem that compounds the problem.
- The middle school years are a time of critical change in the manner of instruction, the learning environment, and the adolescent students themselves.
- Reasonable accommodations required by the Americans with Disabilities Act (ADA) will encourage general classroom accommodations.

Purpose of This Publication

The primary purpose of *I Can Learn* is to provide information and suggestions to teachers, parents, and school principals concerned about children experiencing learning or performance problems in school. Although these children can learn, they differ in their learning abilities or ways of showing what they have learned. The suggestions in this document offer help for enhancing children's abilities, preventing school failure, and remediating a variety of learning difficulties.

Approaches to Children's Difficulties with Learning and Performance

For many years parents and teachers have been concerned about children whose performance in school should be better. Over the years a number of labels have been applied to these children, such as learning disabled, neurologically handicapped, brain-injured, hyperactive, attention deficient, or learning disordered. Recently, the emphasis has been shifted toward understanding the variety of ways in which children receive information, process that information, and show that they have learned the information and can apply it. This approach has been termed the "differing learning abilities" or "different learning styles" approach in contrast to the "learning disability" approach.

Not only are school professionals who specialize in learning disabilities beginning to apply the new "different learning styles" approach; but teachers, parents, and even students are also encouraged to try it.

This more recent approach emphasizes early identification and intervention whenever possible. If a child who is at risk for a learning difficulty is identified by a parent or teacher before academic failures become chronic and if appropriate classroom adaptations and individualized strategies are implemented, the child maintains self-esteem; and the teacher and parent experience less frustration. Children who daily experience more successes than failures in their school setting will continue to take risks and to learn.

The informal identification of behaviors of a child with a learning problem and the resulting classroom adaptations to accommodate that child are not aimed at curing or remediating the problem. Rather, informal identification and implementation of individualized classroom adaptations are directed toward finding out *how* a child learns and *how* a child can best display what he or she has learned. On the basis of that individualized information, the teacher can teach and test; the child can learn, perform, and achieve; and the parent(s) can help the child at home in a way that is consistent with the child's specific learning styles. This individualized information also helps the child to achieve better self-understanding and to develop personal strategies for success in school.

Assessing the difference between academic underachievement and a learning disability, including dyslexia or an attention deficit problem, is difficult and cannot be appropriately done without a formal, professional assessment.

Further, it must be acknowledged that, without expert assistance, teachers and parents cannot help all children, no matter how hard they (and the children) try. Overall, children who experience learning difficulties commonly need a combination of classroom adaptations and individualized compensatory tools and strategies. Some of these children, however, will not benefit sufficiently from adaptations in instruction or from personal strategies alone. Some children will also need specific, professional interventions or remediation.

Children who continue to fail despite classroom adaptations should be referred for assessment (with parental consent). Whether or not the children tested meet California's current eligibility criteria for special education services, teachers and parent(s) need the assessment information and the recommendations of the assessment team to plan for further helpful modifications in the classroom and home as well as to develop successful compensatory tools and strategies. Therefore, the assessment team must focus not only on criteria for eligibility but also on determining the child's learning strengths and weaknesses, information about which can then be clearly and pragmatically communicated to the children's teachers, parent(s), and, when appropriate, to the children themselves.

One important aspect of these current approaches to helping a child with difficulties in learning and performance is the documentation and passing on of information among the child's teachers regarding which adaptations and strategies best benefit a child's learning and retrieval processes. Along these lines, parents should also be encouraged to keep a folder with records of their child's specific needs in the classroom and copies of completed homework.

Scientific, medical, and educational researchers are making steady progress in understanding the variety of ways in which children and adults learn. Users of this document who need more information on specific learning disabilities, dyslexia, attention deficit disorder (ADD), or attention deficit hyperactivity disorder (ADHD), or the latest research regarding multiple learning styles are encouraged to look into the professional literature or to communicate personally with knowledgeable professionals in the field. A list of selected references, including research articles and books, as well as a list of agencies and individuals, is included in the last section of this publication. Teachers, parents, school principals, and other educational professionals are encouraged to update their present understanding of learning differences and styles.

Content and Organization of This Publication

The main body of the document is divided into two parts: Part One, "Cues and Clues" and Part Two, "Gathering the Team—Finding Solutions." Part One contains chapters I, II, and III, which are aimed at the classroom level for particular students about whom a teacher or parent is concerned.

Chapter I, "Characteristic Behaviors and General Interventions," describes the classroom behavior of a child who may be experiencing difficulties in learning or performance. The chapter contains information about general impressions the teacher may form about a child in the classroom. Characteristic behaviors are divided into two main types of difficulties: (1) difficulties in receiving instruction; and (2) difficulties relating to demonstrating performance. Also appearing are lists of general learning difficulties, instructional accommodations to meet the difficulties, strategies for facilitating instructional delivery, and strategies for facilitating performance.

Chapter II, "Specific Characteristics and Interventions," describes difficulties students might have in certain areas, followed by strategies that a classroom teacher can select to help students improve learning or performance. The strategies address ways to facilitate classroom instruction and student learning and performance. Each area contains lists of ideas for the teacher to use in the classroom. "Difficulties and Strategies in Receiving Instruction" contains lists for listening comprehension, decoding (reading) skills, reading comprehension, mathematical reasoning and problem solving, appropriate social skills, organizational skills, and students' attention span. The section entitled "Organizational Skills" is further divided into four subareas: space, priorities, time, and transitions. "Difficulties with and Strategies for Demonstrating Performance" contains lists for verbal expression, handwriting and copying, spelling (encoding), written expression, mathematical computation, retention and retrieval of material presented, reduced productivity, and taking tests.

In Chapter III, "Learning Disabilities and Related Disabilities," concepts are discussed and clarified regarding developmental aphasia, dyslexia, and attention deficits, which encompass attention deficit hyperactivity disorder and attention deficit disorder. An extensive section contains groupings of learning difficulties that dyslexic children frequently experience. Also presented is the four-step process for developing positive behavioral support, followed by the sections titled "Questions and Answers" and "Selected References on Dyslexia."

Part Two, "Gathering the Team—Finding Solutions," consists of three chapters, all containing information related to the concepts and procedures for special education services. Chapter IV, "Referral, Assessment, and Eligibility for Special Education Services," spells out the concepts and procedures of referral and assessment to determine the educational needs of a child experiencing difficulties with learning or performance. Such a child has not benefited from strategies and interventions tried in the general classroom. The federal and state laws and regulations governing referral and assessment of a child for possible special educational services are covered in this chapter, along with a series of commonly asked questions with answers. This chapter also covers the concept of using assessment information to help the student who has experienced difficulties with learning or performance but is not eligible for special education services.

Chapter V, "Planning and Providing Services," describes the concept of providing an IEP for each student who is to receive special education and related services. The procedures for developing an IEP, in cooperation with the student's parent(s), are spelled out; and the content of a student's IEP is described. Appropriate sections of applicable federal and state laws and regulations are cited. The section titled "Questions and Answers" concludes this chapter.

Chapter VI, "Service Delivery Models and Strategies for School Sites," describes the following six special education program options available in California: general education; resource specialist; designated instruction and services; special classes and centers;

nonpublic, nonsectarian school services; and state special schools. Five variations of ways to provide resource specialist services are described as follows: the traditional direct service model, the classroom intervention model, the departmentalized model for students in secondary schools (usually in grades seven through twelve), the consultative/collaborative model, and the school-based coordinated programs model. Also discussed is the flexibility given to schools offering programs under the provisions of the School-Based Coordinated Programs Act of 1981. The section titled "Strategies for School Sites" contains information about schoolwide approaches to enhance the success of all students. Schools can examine those approaches and consider using or adapting the ones that seem the most practical and most promising for the particular school. The approaches are listed as follows:

1. School restructuring
2. Every Student Succeeds, a statewide program
3. School-Based Coordinated Programs Act
4. Student study team
5. Consultation/Collaboration
6. Peer coaching
7. Collaborative in-service training
8. Schoolwide incentives
9. Cross-age tutoring and peer tutoring
10. Articulation between school levels

Answers to several commonly asked questions are provided at the end of this chapter.

The Conclusion contains a summary of the major concepts in this publication and a list of selected references. A list of agencies, advocacy groups, professional groups, and state and national organizations that can provide additional information, appears in Appendix A; and pertinent legal requirements appear in Appendix B. Appendix C, "Characteristics of Children with Attention Disorders," examines the symptoms and behaviors of children with attention deficit hyperactivity disorder and attention deficit disorder. The Glossary contains technical terms appearing in the document and in federal and state laws and regulations. A list of selected references provides sources for persons seeking additional knowledge about the topics examined in this publication.

Uses for the Information in This Publication

This publication is designed to be used in six major ways. First, the information will help parents and school personnel improve their understanding of the needs of students with problems in learning or performance, including learning disabilities, dyslexia, attention deficit disorder, and attention deficit hyperactivity disorder. The information is also intended to help parents and school personnel improve their effectiveness in meeting those students' educational needs.

Second, the information can be used to promote effective instructional techniques for all children. When applied in the classroom, the strategies may be helpful to all students; but they will be absolutely necessary for the success of students with problems in learning or performance.

Third, the document provides references for information and resources to assist parents, teachers, principals, and administrators to improve the effectiveness of instruction and educational programs.

Fourth, the information on characteristic behaviors can be used as one basis for screening students for possible difficulties with learning and performance.

Fifth, the document contains citations for the major federal and state laws and regulations that apply to referral for assessment, determination of eligibility, and provisions of special education and related services to children with specific learning disabilities. Only pertinent sections from the California *Education Code* and from federal laws are included.

Sixth, the document provides information about school practices that help all the students in a school to succeed.

Benefits of Using the Information in This Publication

It is hoped that a variety of benefits and positive outcomes will occur for the following groups that will use this publication and become familiar with its content:

Students

Students (for whom this material is age appropriate) will find information that is directly accessible within the guidelines, detailed, and clearly stated and that pertains to some of the learning difficulties that they experience daily. It is hoped that these students will also discover that teachers and other educational professionals are eager to listen to the students' ideas regarding the best ways for the students to take in and retrieve information. Another hope is that these ideas will be considered carefully when classroom interventions are being developed and put into place. These same students should also find that their feedback is regularly sought to determine the effectiveness of the agreed-on interventions.

Teachers

Teachers will discover that students with specific learning disabilities exhibit many of the characteristic behaviors that also appear in students whose educational needs do not meet the criteria for eligibility for special education services. For instance, "gifted dyslexic" students are often able to compensate well enough in difficult areas so that, although these students fall far short of their intellectual capabilities, their performance seldom lags far enough behind the standards for their appropriate grade level to alert the eligibility assessment team. Furthermore, teachers will find that many of the strategies and interventions that are effective for students with documented learning disabilities will also benefit other students with less severe, but nonetheless legitimate difficulties in school.

Parents

Parents—by studying this document and then reflecting on their knowledge of their children's learning styles, behavior toward homework, and feelings toward school—can actively collaborate with school staff to ensure that the educational program in which their children are enrolled best suits their unique learning and performance needs.

School Districts

School districts will find that by using this document as part of their staff development program for regular education teachers and other personnel, they can make staff members more aware of problems in learning and in demonstrating mastery of material, as well as of new ways to implement instructional adaptations in regular education classrooms.

School Leaders

School leaders will find a greater variety of ways to organize instructional programs to meet the educational needs of many students experiencing difficulties in school. Some of these students are being served exclusively by general education, some by special education, and some by a combination of services.

Limitations of This Publication

The strategies in this publication are to be used as a resource bank or a set of tools that may assist teachers, parents, principals, and administrators in meeting the challenge of providing effective instruction for all children. Other specific strategies or service delivery methods may be as successful or more successful in meeting the needs of a particular student. This document does not completely resolve all of the problems encountered by students whose learning abilities and modes of classroom performance differ.

No specific strategy exists that will meet the unique abilities and disabilities of all learners. Nor is there a particular service delivery model that will meet the unique assets and challenges of each school site.

This document does not contain specific procedures to be followed. Since all students are individuals, combinations of these strategies, allowing for multiple aspects of development, may be necessary before the appropriate accommodation or intervention is found. The information in this document has been culled from the collective experience of many professionals and parents who have worked with students experiencing learning difficulties in school.

Questions and Answers

Is the information in this document consistent with state and federal mandates established in federal and state laws and regulations?

Yes, the information is consistent with federal and state mandates but does not include all laws governing the administration and operation of special educational and related services provided for children with disabilities such as specific learning disabilities. The federal and state mandates are to be carried out by school districts, county offices of education, and Special Education Local Plan Areas (SELPAs) so that students with exceptional needs participate in free and appropriate programs that meet their special educational needs.

Where appropriate, the pertinent portions of federal and state laws and regulations are included. Examples of federal laws are the Individuals with Disabilities Education Act (IDEA), the Americans with Disabilities Act (ADA), and the Vocational Rehabilitation Act.

Where can I find copies of the state laws that were mentioned in this chapter?

See *California Special Education Programs: A Composite of Laws* (Sixteenth edition). Sacramento: California Department of Education, 1994. This publication, which covers state laws enacted through 1993, is available at no charge but in limited quantities from the Bureau of Publications, Sales Unit, California Department of Education, P.O. Box 271, Sacramento, CA 95812-0271. This publication is revised annually.

Where can I find copies of the federal laws and regulations?

Many but not all local public libraries and school district libraries have reference copies for use. You should telephone to find out whether copies are available. The most useful information on IDEA is found in the *Code of Federal Regulations: CFR* 34, Parts 300 to 399. Copies can be purchased from the Superintendent of Documents, U.S. Government Printing Office, Washington, DC 20402-9328; telephone (202) 783-3238. *(Note*: The *CFR* is expensive, with parts 300–399 costing about $20. The Americans with Disabilities Act [ADA] and Section 504 are not included in those parts.)

PART ONE

Cues
and Clues

CHAPTER I

Characteristic Behaviors and General Interventions

Τhis chapter describes some general *classroom behaviors that may indicate a student's need for attention. The difference between the student's problems in receiving instruction and the student's performance as a result of instruction is emphasized. General strategies are listed to accommodate for a student's difficulties.*

Background Information

A number of criteria distinguish the child with a potential learning disorder, including dyslexia and attention deficits, from children with other educational needs. (*Dyslexia* is a disorder in learning the written or symbol language skills of reading, writing, and spelling through conventional instruction. See Chapter III for a more extensive discussion of dyslexia.) This document was prepared to assist children *who seem as if they should be doing better in school.* Their academic performance differs from the judgments of parents, teachers, and other professionals about the child's innate scholastic potential. Because the discrepancy between the potential and performance of some children is not significant enough for them to qualify for special education services, other ways must be found to meet those children's needs.

Parents and professionals need to understand that although children do not qualify for special education services, they still need help with academic work and *cannot nor should not be expected to perform just like other students in the class.* Symptoms of learning difficulties range from mild to severe. One cannot observe a recognized, identifiable point at which children have a specific learning disability, dyslexia, or attention deficit disorder. Assessing the difference between a learning disability and underachievement is difficult.

Several key dimensions can be considered when children are being assessed, including the cause of the learning difficulty and the severity, pervasiveness, and duration of the problem. The interrelationship of these factors affects the type of interventions that are most effective for each child. California has developed specific criteria that formalize the identification of learning disabilities and enable a child to become eligible to receive special education services. A thorough description of this process appears in Chapter IV, "Referral, Assessment, and Eligibility for Special Education Services." Some children may exhibit learning difficulties only with certain kinds of tasks or in certain classes. **These children need accommodations in their instruction or performance or both if they are to have a fair opportunity to show what they know in each of their subjects.**

Content and Organization of This Chapter

This chapter is organized into sections on "Receiving Instruction and Demonstrating Performance," "General Learning Difficulties," "Selecting Accommodations," "General Strategies for Facilitating Instructional Delivery," and "General Strategies for Facilitating Students' Performance." The topics in each section are examined in depth.

General classroom learning behaviors and problems that may appear in children with learning difficulties are described in this chapter. The mere recognition of these symptoms by teachers or parents does not, however, constitute a valid diagnosis of a child's specific learning disability, including dyslexia and attention deficits. Indeed, some of the specific behaviors described may be developmentally appropriate at certain ages. As scholastic demands on children change (for example, according to grade level), some behaviors observed in a particular child may seem to abate, and new ones will appear unexpectedly. This pattern frequently appears in children whose school performance is inconsistent. The descriptions of common learning problems children encounter enable parents and teachers to determine jointly which accommodations in the classroom would help the children to succeed.

The learning problems discussed in this chapter are behaviors of children with general learning difficulties. Chapter II lists behaviors common in children having problems with receiving instruction and addresses characteristics of children with problems demonstrating performance. Readers must **not** assume that the characteristics listed define that disorder. **Formal identification of each of the characteristics described in the sections must be determined by an appropriate assessment team of clinicians.** However, recognition of certain characteristics by parents and teachers justifies the implementation of appropriate accommodations in instruction or performance or both.

To help students not performing at expected levels, teachers can implement certain performance-based accommodations in the classroom. The accommodations do help a child to show what he or she knows but are not designed to modify the behavioral objectives developed for a particular learning activity. The teacher's informal recognition that a child has a mild learning problem is the basis for implementing accommodations. Mild learning problems are not likely to warrant a child's being placed in special education. Nevertheless, students need adjustments in the delivery of instruction and in the ways they can demonstrate their knowledge and actively participate.

The accommodations presented minimally intrude on a teacher's planning time and instructional delivery. Frequently, teachers have expressed concern about whether providing individual accommodations is reasonable or fair. The validity of implementing these accommodations when necessary is based on the premise that educators try to give each student what he or she needs in order to learn and perform successfully. Recently enacted laws have supported students with visible physical disabilities or known learning disabilities or both to gain improved access to the learning opportunities available in the mainstream classroom. Special physical or procedural adaptations or both enable these individuals to realize their potential; for example, the use of computer technology with appropriate adaptive devices. The accommodations presented extend that effort to students with milder and less visible learning problems.

The material in chapters I, II, and III was developed for three specific purposes:

1. To promote the general education teacher's knowledge of classroom accommodations that have been successfully implemented

2. To enable general education teachers to select specific accommodations that are directly relevant to a particular student's needs for instruction or performance

3. To make students and parents aware of accommodations and interventions so that they may effectively ask for appropriate help

Receiving Instruction and Demonstrating Performance

When a student does not demonstrate skills taught in the classroom, one generally assumes that the student does not comprehend the material being taught. However, with learning disabled students a dramatic discrepancy can exist between comprehension of information and the ability to demonstrate that understanding. Different combinations of behavior may indicate variations in patterns of strengths and weaknesses in language learning. Sometimes what we observe may seem to be contradictory. Some typical examples are as follows:

1. A student for whom handwriting is a painful, frustrating experience is often a talented artist capable of creating detailed, sophisticated drawings.
2. A child who can play a complex piece of music after hearing it only a few times may have problems discriminating individual sounds within words.
3. A student who is capable of giving an intricate explanation of genetics (learned from conversations with her mother) may not be able to spell well because of difficulties with auditory sequencing.

Many students can explain complex concepts orally but are unable to express the same ideas adequately in writing. This problem is not necessarily the result of laziness. The discrepancy between oral and written expression may be commonly seen in students who experience difficulties in processing information through sensory experiences. Students with facility in oral skills are fortunate. Their intelligence is obvious, and the discrepancy between their oral and written expression, although frustrating, can be easily observed.

Other students may be capable of understanding all that is said to them yet be unable to articulate (speak/say) what they know. Knowledge of this difficulty is important because those students' inability to respond orally may seem to indicate a lack of understanding. In such cases it is important to provide alternative ways of demonstrating comprehension of information.

A student may be skilled at repairing bicycles or even cars yet be unable to read the instructions for performing such a task. This is an example of a student who learns easily through observation or listening or both but may be unable to acquire knowledge by reading. The competence of this student may not be recognized or rewarded in school.

Other students may have great difficulties understanding spoken language. Concepts may be grasped very slowly or lost—requiring much repetition. The child may *appear* to be dull, uninterested, or inattentive. By the *time* the child organizes the verbal input well enough to get the meaning, the speaker may have moved on too fast for the listening child to keep pace. The concept can be lost entirely despite the child's ability to comprehend. Unless additional time is allowed and an opportunity to rehear spoken words is given, the concept is lost.

Children who are verbose often have difficulty getting to the point. They may have problems with syntax (order of words in a statement), grammar, phrasing, organization, and recall of the appropriate words needed to express their thoughts. It may seem as if these children do not know what they are trying to say when, in fact, they are having difficulty recalling specific words to explain what is understood and organized conceptually.

The strengths and abilities of these groups of children are usually not visible. The children rarely excel on group tests or in any activity in which performance depends on quick perception and comprehension of directions that must be followed by performance within time limits. Their intellectual potential is often underestimated.

General Learning Difficulties

Teachers in a classroom may notice some of the characteristic behaviors listed in the section that follows. The two main types of impressions a teacher gains from noting such behaviors are that a student has difficulties in (1) receiving instruction; and (2) expressing what he or she knows or has learned as a result of instruction. Those difficulties need to be differentiated from the difficulties a student has in interacting with his or her peers.

The characteristic behaviors to observe are:

1. The student is academically struggling, frustrated, or anxious. For example, he or she may clown, act up or act out, or daydream; may appear lazy, unmotivated, or inattentive; may seem not to be trying; or may be unhappy or have low self-esteem.
2. The student seems to possess adequate intelligence but performs inconsistently and below expectations.
3. The student shows exaggerated and seemingly mysterious variance in performance and knowledge retention and seems to have unexplainable gaps in skills.
4. The student finds organizing materials and managing time difficult.
5. The student has difficulty in completing tasks requiring two or more simultaneous activities, such as listening to a lecture and taking notes, or requiring sequencing ability, such as following multistep oral directions.
6. The student's response time to directives seems inappropriate; that is, either too rapid (impulsive) or too slow.
7. The student frequently forgets or does not turn in homework.
8. The student may feel overwhelmed with the amount of information presented in visual, oral, and written form.

Selecting Accommodations

To facilitate practical use of this chapter, teachers can use the sequence listed below to determine which accommodations best fit the student's instructional or performance needs.

Teachers can do the following:

1. Record observations of a student's perceived learning and performance strengths and weaknesses signaled by "General Learning Difficulties."
2. Review the sections titled, "General Strategies for Facilitating Instructional Delivery" and "General Strategies for Facilitating Students' Performance."
3. Identify, on the basis of your in-class observations, the area or areas that are the most difficult for the student (see Table 1 in Chapter II).
4. Turn to the sections in Chapter II that specifically outline suggested accommodations and select those that seem the most appropriate from your observation of the student and knowledge of your classroom.
5. List the accommodations you have selected, review them for inconsistencies, target one area to start, and record the results.

General Strategies for Facilitating Instructional Delivery

The classroom accommodations listed in this section are for teachers with students who have difficulty receiving instruction. The accommodations are designed to facilitate the communication of information, concepts, and skills when students have difficulty comprehending new material.

General strategies for facilitating instructional delivery are listed as follows:

1. **Relate new concepts to a student's background, experience, and interests** so that students will perceive the relevance of the material.
2. **Clarify intended outcomes** for a lesson when each new study unit is begun. Then go back and present each skill component singularly and sequentially, assessing often to ascertain a student's mastery. This procedure will help you, the teacher, to pinpoint more specifically where a breakdown in comprehension occurs and provide much-needed structure and organization of lessons.
3. **Review frequently** and integrate new material with previously presented concepts to facilitate transfer from a student's short-term memory to long-term memory. Study done in a meaningful and relevant context will significantly enhance the effectiveness of a review.
4. **Use simultaneous, multisensory instructional strategies** as often as possible. Combine visual-auditory-kinesthetic presentations.
5. **Use manipulative or hands-on materials** to supplement instruction of new concepts and to evoke students' responses.
6. **Consider altering the format** of written handouts to reduce the amount of material in the student's visual field. Use underlining or shading to highlight the most important concepts. Separate work sheets into manageable segments. For example, when constructing quizzes, put no more than six match-up items or items requiring filling in blanks with vocabulary words in any section.
7. **List targeted vocabulary words** at the top of a page on all fill-in-the-blanks or extended written exercises.
8. **Use simple mnemonic (memory) devices** to facilitate retention of facts to be memorized; for example, for teaching directions, **N**orth, **E**ast, **S**outh, or **W**est, give a cue phrase like **N**ever **E**at **S**our **W**heat.

9. **Use graphic displays and diagrams** whenever possible to show the relationships among ideas and to help students organize newly presented ideas and concepts. Demonstrating use of media will provide students with initial understanding of how they can use these materials to demonstrate their knowledge.

10. **Allow students time to prepare their answers.** Pose a question and then, before asking students to respond, engage in a short time-buying activity like erasing the board to make room for recording students' responses.

11. Have a private conversation with a student to develop a "secret code" that will signal when he or she will be called on during a class discussion. This activity will **alleviate anxiety** of students about **being spontaneously called on** and will enable them to concentrate on information or concepts being presented during a discussion.

12. **Allow students to take difficult subjects as intensive study during the summer** rather than as part of the regular year's course load. Even within this context, accommodations in instruction and performance may be necessary. (For example, studying a foreign language can be difficult for some students. Delaying the introduction of the study of foreign language may be advisable.)

13. **Use computer technology** to individualize instruction, to create individualized materials, to enhance the writing process, to provide multimodality instruction, and to provide a variety of formats for presentation and interaction. Computers are especially useful for students with dyslexia.

General Strategies for Facilitating Students' Performance

These accommodations will facilitate the performance of students by helping them to demonstrate their degree of knowledge acquisition when their oral or written language capacity may be compromised. The purpose of this section is to describe methods that most teachers have already used in their classrooms and to provide further alternatives to measure and foster students' acquisition of knowledge.

General strategies for facilitating students' performance are listed as follows:

1. Provide students with possible learning difficulties with varying degrees and types of support. Classroom teachers should be guided by the principle of **providing what certain students *need* to be successful** instead of being governed by the principle that "sameness for all is the only fair way." In that respect "study buddies," peer tutors, and collaborative learning activities should be considered as part of the program. These supportive techniques will enhance the opportunity for certain students to show what they know and to participate, perform, and succeed in classroom activities.

2. Design student activities that **simultaneously stimulate as many senses as possible.** In addition to providing written responses, students can respond through verbal and large-motor modalities; for example, through pantomiming, role-playing, or character simulations.

3. Provide students with **additional time to prepare or respond or do both.** This accommodation is one of the most valued for students. The process of receiving, organizing, or expressing the language component of targeted skills is frequently

the source of students' learning struggles. Examples of alternative strategies for students who need more time to complete and succeed with tasks are to:

a. Provide for extended time as follows: before school, after school, at lunchtime, during recess, during time between classes, during Saturday school, or during homeroom period.
b. Collaborate with other teachers.
c. Use instructional assistants.
d. Place students in a less distracting environment; for example, in the library or the school office.
e. Provide take-home tests with a parent as monitor.
f. Provide older peer monitors; for example, honor students.
g. Reduce the number of test items.
h. Use computers, tape recorders, or videos.
i. Allow students with shortened days to return or remain at school for extended time. For example, these students might be in a regional occupational program (ROP) or a work experience education program.
j. Ask a volunteer parent to monitor a student's work.
k. Provide study partners.
l. Provide a means of assessment other than timed paper-and-pencil tests.

4. **Present mistakes as a potential learning opportunity,** not as wrong behavior. Create a safe environment in which all students can make mistakes. Active participation and risk-taking enable teachers to observe children's strengths in learning and sources of their weaknesses in learning.
5. Provide students with opportunities for **immediate self-checking on independent exercises.** Modeling a correct answer at the beginning or end of an exercise helps students monitor their own work and make some corrections in their work before handing in assignments.
6. **Allow students to clarify or explain** the rationale for their answers. Although their answer may not be the intended one, allow them to explain the reasons for their response before determining their degree of error.
7. **Provide adaptations of well-known board or television games** like Trivial Pursuit or Jeopardy to reinforce newly introduced skills or concepts creatively and effectively.
8. Facilitate the use of **computer technology.** Students' use of word processors enhances the writing process and encourages editing and revision. Many other computer programs are designed to provide immediate feedback, including remediation, and multiple formats. Additionally, computers allow students to develop the ability to generalize as they apply specific skills to simulations. Similarly, tape recorders and calculators are useful to some students in overcoming problems with receptivity and inattention.

Summary

Students experiencing learning difficulties often manifest a confusing array of strengths as well as weaknesses. Frequently, a student who is struggling academically seems talented and successful at one task or in one situation, yet another seemingly similar task causes that same student great frustration and difficulty.

When students experience difficulties, appropriate strategies need to be initiated. Three ways to assist students are:

1. Accommodations. The general classroom environment, classroom procedures, methods of presenting instruction, and techniques of eliciting responses from students are adapted or modified to improve students' achievement.
2. Compensatory tools and technology. Assistive technology such as computers with appropriate software, calculators, videos, and other media are used to provide needed information and alternative means for students to respond.
3. Direct instruction in basic skills. Alternative teaching, cooperative learning, and individualized programs are used to promote development in basic skills for students who have difficulty learning this material through conventional classroom instruction.

CHAPTER II

Specific Characteristics and Interventions

This section informs parents and provides teachers with classroom modifications that will enable students to receive instruction from teachers more effectively. Alternative means are provided through which students may demonstrate a truer degree of skill or acquisition of concepts or both. The interventions are provided for situations in which many different learning approaches may exist among students.

Organization of Material

The characteristic classroom behaviors and interventions presented in this chapter are organized so that the material on any page can be separated and used as a discussion and planning aid by a teacher and parent, as a focal point for teacher collaboration, or as material for staff development purposes. Each page lists difficulties (characteristics) on one side and strategies (interventions) on the reverse. The pages follow the sequence in Table 1.

The first topic in the table is "Listening Comprehension." That topic begins the series in which difficulties are listed on one side of the page and strategies on the reverse. Next will follow "Decoding (Reading) Skills" and so on through the list of the areas of receiving instruction. The pages then continue with the areas of demonstrating performance. By referring to Table 1, the reader can put together those pages believed to be the most appropriate for any individual student.

Table 1
Overview of Students' Problems in Regular Classrooms

Receiving	Demonstrating
Listening comprehension	Verbal expression
Decoding (reading) skills	Handwriting and copying
Reading comprehension	Spelling (encoding)
Mathematical reasoning and problem solving	Written expression
Appropriate social skills	Mathematical computation
Organizational skills	Retention and retrieval of material presented
Students' attention span	Reduced productivity
	Taking tests

Difficulties with and Strategies for Receiving Instruction

The next section examines areas in which students may have difficulties with receiving instruction: listening comprehension, decoding (reading) skills, reading comprehension, mathematical reasoning and problem solving, appropriate social skills, organizational skills, and students' attention span. Difficulties students may have in each of these areas are listed, followed by strategies to help students. The pages in this chapter may be removed from this publication to facilitate their use for discussion.

Listening Comprehension

Difficulties   Listening is probably the skill most frequently demanded of children both at home and in school. Adults often perceive a child as being purposefully inattentive when in fact he or she has not fully understood a lengthy oral message or has been unable to remain attentive during oral presentations. The following behaviors are often displayed by children who are having difficulty processing, attending to, or understanding verbal instruction:

1. Appears to lose interest or attention during oral presentations
2. May seem to daydream or to become restless when listening is required
3. Has difficulty in remembering things that are told to him or her
4. Has difficulty in following orally conveyed, sequenced directions
5. Requests the teacher or a classmate to repeat directions or facts just presented
6. Looks to see what others are doing directly after multistep directions have been given
7. Gives answers that seem unrelated to the questions asked
8. Appears to be easily distracted by background noise
9. Appears unable to listen and write notes simultaneously

Listening Comprehension

General strategies for facilitating a student's listening comprehension are listed as follows:

1. Seat the student so that he or she can hear the teacher clearly. Avoid seating the student near chronically distracting noises, such as near a heater or fish tank.
2. Select a student who consistently writes complete and legible notes to act as a scribe. This procedure will allow the students with difficulties in listening comprehension to attend fully to the presentation. The scribe can be provided with carbon paper or carbonless lined paper; or at the end of each class, a photocopy can be made of the scribe's notes.
3. Create and adhere to a specific structure regarding how and when assignments will be given and explained. For example, some teachers give the homework assignment at the beginning of class. The assignment is always written on the upper right-hand corner of the board, and time is allowed for students to copy the assignment and to ask clarifying questions. This consistent classroom structure is helpful for students who are experiencing learning difficulties.
4. Keep oral directions simple. Present directions one step at a time.
5. Accompany verbal directions and presentations, whenever possible, with written directions, a written outline, or a visual model. The student should be able to see these visual aids throughout the classroom activity.
6. Augment a presentation by frequently using visual props and aids. Supplement lectures with audiovisual presentations and hands-on activities.
7. Write key terms and concepts on the board as you introduce them in your presentation.
8. Give alert cues, such as "Really pay attention; this is important," when you are about to deliver important oral directions.
9. Be conscious of your rate of speech and speak more slowly if keeping up seems difficult for students. Gesturing and varying the volume and pitch of your voice can also help students listen closely.
10. Allow a student to repeat or paraphrase directions to ascertain whether he or she understands them clearly.
11. Interject independent, quiet visual-motor activities periodically during your presentation to provide students with a short respite from listening.
12. Allow a study partner to interpret directions for a student at the beginning of any independent practice exercises. It often helps if time is allowed for the student experiencing listening difficulties to reiterate verbally his or her understanding of the directions.
13. Allow students to work in small groups, an activity that will facilitate the acquisition of information you want students to retain.
14. Realize that some students can listen only if they are doodling or are engaged in other motor activities. Limit the student's distractibility to others and help the student channel a need for motor involvement.

Decoding (Reading) Skills

Difficulties   One of the most important skills a child must learn in school is *decoding,* the ability to look at a group of letters and be able to say or think accurately the word that it represents. For many reasons children might exhibit difficulties when attempting to acquire this skill. They may have a learning disability, such as dyslexia. They may be working in their second language, a process that creates confusion regarding specific phonemes. They may not have been maturationally ready for instruction in decoding when it was offered in earlier grades. Whatever the cause, an inability to decode efficiently represents a substantial barrier to learning. Children who are having difficulty learning and applying decoding skills often display the following behaviors:

1. Have difficulty in identifying or remembering or both the names and sequence of the letters of the alphabet.
2. Have difficulty in learning how to blend sounds to form words.
3. Have difficulty in learning and remembering high-use sight words, such as *they, was, from, one, said,* and *have.*
4. Seem embarrassed or reluctant to read aloud in class.
5. Demonstrate many reading inaccuracies with letters and words when reading aloud. May make errors—such as letter reversals *(b* and *d)*; letter transpositions *(was* and *saw)*; letter inversions *(m* and *w);* word omissions (drops such words as *and, a, the, for, to*); letter omissions *(steet* for *street, pace* for *place,* or *can* for *cane)*—or may make additions, substitutions, or mispronunciations of words and letters.
6. May read aloud with a choppy, hesitant cadence.
7. May frequently lose their place when reading or using their finger or a ruler to keep their place in material being studied.
8. May be unable to read homework assignments without parental assistance.
9. May express a lack of interest in or even a dislike of reading.
10. Does not read for pleasure.

Decoding (Reading) Skills

Strategies   Students experiencing difficulties in acquiring decoding skills will usually require several types of interventions. Direct instruction in the mechanics of written language is an essential intervention toward effective building of decoding skills. The student with difficulties in decoding will require and benefit from classroom instruction in the mechanics of reading as well as from classroom modifications and the use of tools and strategies while basic skills are being built. These adaptations and tools are listed as follows:

1. Provide extended time for students to complete tests and reading and writing assignments—an essential need for students for whom decoding (reading) is a problem.
2. Combine instruction in phonics with instruction in literature.
3. Teach the often overlapping principles that govern decoding and spelling; for example, the spelling rule for silent -*e,* rules for syllabication, and roots and affixes.
4. Ensure that the student is offered a selection of books within the student's reading level so that he or she can do individualized reading assignments.
5. Do not require a student with poor decoding skills to read aloud in front of classmates.
6. Consider reduced homework assignments while the student is gaining decoding skills.
7. Support the use of tape-recorded books. Provide the student's parents with a complete list of books to be assigned. They will need to know the title of the book, the author, the publisher, the date published, and the edition.
8. Encourage use of computers with appropriate programs for children with deficits in reading. Use of computers will enhance students' understanding of the connection between reading and writing. Although formal instruction in keyboarding is helpful, it is not a prerequisite to the implementation of this technology. Some videos are helpful when words are screened along with visual presentations.

Reading Comprehension

Difficulties   Children who have difficulties with reading comprehension often fall into one of several categories. Some children struggle with decoding, a difficulty that adversely affects their reading comprehension. For this type of child, direct instruction in decoding (word attack) skills will often automatically increase their reading comprehension.

However, some children may decode fairly accurately but seem unable to recall or understand the message they have just read. These difficulties in reading comprehension are not related to difficulties with decoding (word attack) skills.

Some children may be working in their second language and may lack automatic decoding skills as well as vocabulary development necessary for reading comprehension.

No matter what the cause, children with deficits in reading comprehension will have difficulties with remembering facts; sequencing pertinent details; and perceiving main ideas, themes, or other inferentially based written information.

Children who are having difficulties in comprehending what they have read often display the following behaviors:

1. Identify the main ideas from material they have read but do not recall pertinent details to support a position. (For example, they might remember that the Prince found Cinderella and that they lived happily ever after but may miss the importance of the glass slipper.)
2. Recall details but cannot summarize them cohesively or identify a theme correctly.
3. Work too slowly or too rapidly on reading assignments.
4. Show differences in understanding material read orally and silently.
5. Fail to use context clues.
6. Read word for word and not in meaningful phrases.
7. Display poor vocabulary when responding orally or in writing.
8. Are unable to relate new information to material learned previously.

A student who decodes adequately or well and still displays difficulties in reading comprehension may require direct instruction in various aspects of comprehension skills, such as vocabulary development, the use of semantics (cues for meaning), and syntax (structural cues in a phrase, clause, or sentence).

Reading Comprehension

Strategies A student experiencing difficulties in reading comprehension because of poor decoding (word attack) skills will require direct instruction in the mechanics (that is, the phonics) of written language.

Use of the following classroom adaptations should facilitate reading comprehension:

1. Relate major concepts in reading material to a student's experiences and interests.
2. Use diagrams or models to reduce the length or wordiness of written directions.
3. Record the new words in a permanent place when you are introducing vocabulary. Next to each word write a familiar synonym for easy reference.
4. Plan the format for discussions to accentuate concepts students need to retain.
5. Pair students for reading assignments when the lesson focuses on acquisition of information. Delegate oral reading to students who are strong in that skill.
6. Encourage students to highlight, underline, and box critical parts of material being presented or to write in the margins of extra textbooks they have purchased. The teacher may even model highlighting techniques in a textbook from which a student can copy so that the student's attention is directed to the important parts.
7. Use asterisks or exclamation points or other distinctive symbols to draw a student's attention to the most important points or steps being presented.
8. Be aware of the quality of photocopied materials. Is the print legible? Are the size of the type and spacing of the text appropriate? Could the contrast cause eyestrain? (Consider photocopying work sheets on off-white or pale colored paper to reduce eyestrain.) Is the student required to read one side of the photocopied material and match up answers from the reverse side? (Often such back-and-forth matching further confuses a student who is already experiencing difficulties with reading comprehension.)
9. Block out information displayed on commercially prepared materials that is not relevant to the completion of the exercise.
10. Show a video or film of literature being read and discuss it in class before and during the reading assignment.
11. Teach the structure of different types of written materials. (For example, explain the difference between a piece of journalism and a mystery novel.)
12. Play in-class games with parts of speech. (For example, how many different verbs can the class offer that relate to human movement? Can the class construct a story by using these action words?)
13. Familiarize students with symbols from a pronunciation guide. Then provide a sheet with new vocabulary and difficult words phonetically coded to help increase the accuracy of students' reading. This method is especially helpful if a reading assignment is lengthy and expected to be completed independently.
14. Go over specific vocabulary before and during the reading assignment if the material to be read includes abstract, foreign, or arcane language (for example, unfamiliar references and terms in Shakespeare's works).
15. Use computers with software programs that focus on skills in vocabulary and reading comprehension. Some software programs also offer speech enhancement to provide a multimodal or multisensory learning environment for the student.

Mathematical Reasoning and Problem Solving

Difficulties   Children who have difficulty in understanding the numerical system or knowing which operations to use or both have problems with mathematical reasoning. It is difficult for children to know whether their answers are wrong if they do not have a realistic picture of how to manipulate quantities. Children for whom mathematical reasoning and problem solving are difficult have the following problems:

1. Difficulty in identifying which arithmetic operations to use with word problems (They are unable to recognize terms associated with mathematical operations; for example, "all together" usually signals addition or multiplication.)
2. Inability to perceive which operation to use if a variable is changed
3. Need for assistance to see repetitive or predictable patterns when they are computing with a certain variable
4. Ability to memorize basic arithmetic facts but difficulty in estimating and regrouping
5. Difficulty in understanding proportions and relative size, especially in fractions and decimals (For example, they have difficulty in understanding **why** the larger the denominator in a fraction, the smaller the slice of the pie.)
6. Confusion in trying to interpret data contained on charts or graphs

Mathematical Reasoning and Problem Solving

Strategies   General strategies for facilitating mathematical reasoning and problem solving are listed as follows:

1. Use manipulatives whenever possible. Students should explore and master concepts with manipulatives before they use paper, pencils, and calculators to perform mathematical computations. Make the transition from manipulative operations to paper-and-pencil tasks in small, precise steps. Do not rush the students. Encourage the use of manipulatives for as long as the students find them helpful.

2. Use color coding and manipulatives to help students who display problems with directionality and sequencing. (*Directionality* refers to the direction of reading from left to right and of doing *mathematics* problems from right to left in addition, subtraction, and multiplication and from left to right in long division. It also refers to vertical directionality as in subtraction and long division. Left-to-right directionality can also be an issue in working with positive and negative numbers as well as with decimal manipulations.) Using different colors for positive and negative numbers can help students understand directionality. Also, relating use of manipulatives to steps in computations can help the student to determine the proper direction to proceed. A color-coded number line displayed in the classroom is also helpful. (*Sequencing* refers to the order of steps to be completed in a process.) Manipulatives, drawings, or diagrams can be used to help students who are confused about sequencing.

3. Help students to solve word problems by first introducing individual small phrases with a discussion of how a phrase can be expressed in the mathematical language of numbers and symbols for operations. Particular emphasis should be given to selecting the specific words that indicate the mathematical operation to be performed. (For example, words like *less than* typically represent subtraction.) Gradually, a list of these words and phrases should be developed and posted for the student's reference. These phrases should be slowly transformed into simple one-operation problems. These problems should then be read aloud in class, and attention should be centered on breaking down each phrase individually into mathematical language.

4. Ask the students to prepare word problems of their own illustrating the use of specified operations after simple one-operation problems have been mastered. Only after these have been mastered should multioperational problems be presented.

5. Organize students in pairs and have them create word problems with statements that can be written, spoken, or drawn. The pairs can then exchange and solve problems.

6. Develop relevant, meaningful problems that students can relate to their background, experiences, and interests.

7. Read a word problem; then ask students to sketch a picture or demonstrate with a manipulative the situation presented.

8. Post in full view of the class a written or pictorial sequence chart that shows steps for solving problems.

9. Provide a model of a completed problem at the top of assigned work sheets.

10. Use manipulatives liberally to accentuate students' opportunities to count. This activity helps students establish a sense of relative proportion and size.

11. Have students demonstrate mastery of concepts by using manipulatives first. This is an excellent paired-student activity. One student reads a problem while a partner arranges manipulatives to show an understanding of the problem.

12. Assign students to reteach a unit, procedure, or process. Students' attitudes should be closely monitored to prevent any embarrassment or ridicule.

13. Provide extra processing time for students who display problems with mathematical reasoning and problem solving. These students benefit from reduced homework assignments (for example, assign every other or every third problem) and from extended time on tests. If providing extended time is not feasible, the students should be graded only on the problems that they were able to complete during the testing period.

14. Allow and encourage the use of a calculator for class work, homework assignments, and tests. Using this device will allow the student to concentrate on problem solving and mathematical reasoning rather than on computation.

15. Facilitate and encourage the use of computer-assisted instruction with software programs that focus on problem solving and, in particular, on simulations that provide students with opportunities to apply their skills.

Appropriate Social Skills

Difficulties   Some children who have problems with social skills will often misunderstand the situation in which they are participating. Their inappropriate behavior is often misinterpreted as purposeful or malicious or both when, in fact, they do not understand how to interact appropriately; or they have missed essential social cues, body language, or subtle verbal messages. Children having problems with social skills may:

1. Misinterpret or be unaware of nonverbal language cues; for example, gestures, facial expressions, or tone of voice.
2. Violate unintentionally the space of others by standing too close when conversing but react with hostility when their own space is encroached on.
3. Talk repeatedly about a single topic during discussion and seem not to understand when the receiver becomes bored or frustrated.
4. Engage in attention-seeking behaviors that are out-of-step with the unspoken patterns or limits of that peer group.
5. Have difficulty integrating into and then maintaining ties with peer groups.
6. Seem not to be in tune with peers' interests, attire, or circumstances and therefore initiate irrelevant conversation that elicits mockery and ridicule.
7. Find fault quickly, often blaming others, and be likely to turn in any individual who has violated a rule.

Appropriate Social Skills

Strategies   Some students with specific learning problems may also behave inappropriately in the classroom or with their peers. These students may have difficulty perceiving social situations realistically. The inappropriate behavior of such students represents a *symptom* of their misunderstanding of social situations and is not the primary source of their problems in the classroom. The following recommendations come from procedures that teachers have reported as helpful for students who behave inappropriately:

1. Strive to improve students' understanding of their behaviors and perceptions of others. Once a teacher knows that students are aware of social and behavioral issues, it is more likely that he or she can develop strategies to alleviate interference from students.

2. Encourage a student to play or socialize with one or two other students at a time rather than trying to integrate him or her into an established large peer group. This strategy will lessen the likelihood that the student will commit a social mistake resulting in ostracism or ridicule from the peer group.

3. Schedule a private conference with the student (after a cooling-off period if necessary) and allow the student to explain from his or her point of view the events that led up to and occurred during the incident. The purpose of this kind of conference is to determine the accuracy of the student's or teacher's perception of the incident and to give the teacher an opportunity to correct any misperceptions.

4. Ask questions that require a student to explain his or her role in the incident instead of reinterpreting the event for him or her. Learning from mistakes will more likely occur if a student acknowledges his or her role or responsibility for the incident.

5. Allow the child to suggest disciplinary repercussions for repeated bad behavior once he or she acknowledges participation and, hopefully, some responsibility. Once the teacher and child have agreed on consequences for repeated bad behavior, record and file the agreement in the presence of the student.

6. Follow through with the student-initiated disciplinary measure if the behavior in question should reappear.

7. Work with the class or group to reduce peer teasing or ostracism.

Organizational Skills

Difficulties   In this section four problems students have with organizational skills will be examined: space, priorities, time, and transitions.

1. *Space.* Students who have difficulty with spatial organization:
   a. Demonstrate poor organization of work on paper, especially when doing mathematical computation or taking notes.
   b. Chronically misplace or forget homework, pencils, books, and other class materials.
   c. Have messy, disorganized notebooks or other materials or messy desks, rooms, or lockers.

2. *Priorities.* Students who have difficulty organizing priorities:
   a. Have difficulty in getting started on assignments.
   b. Have trouble with making choices and identifying priorities.
   c. Become easily distracted by extraneous stimuli and are often deterred from working on tasks.

3. *Time.* Students who have difficulty in organizing time:
   a. Chronically lose track of time and always seem to do things at the last minute.
   b. Have difficulty with time management and in recalling when and where an event of perceived importance occurred.
   c. Regularly put things off until the last minute and then become panicky.

4. *Transitions.* Students who have difficulty in making transitions:
   a. Do not know where to begin or how to recognize a good stopping point when undertaking a project.
   b. Become disoriented and have difficulty in adjusting to changes in routine.
   c. Have difficulty in settling down and becoming focused after making a transition from one activity to another or from one subject to another.

Organizational Skills

Strategies   General strategies for facilitating the students' ability to organize are listed as follows:

1. Establish and adhere to a daily routine in your classroom and post a daily schedule in either written or pictorial form.
2. Post and use organizational aids such as calendars and schedules.
3. At the beginning of each study unit, provide the students with a calendar depicting due dates for all work to be assigned.
4. Provide students with a study guide depicting important terms and key questions that focus on the concepts you want the class to remember.
5. Develop with the students a self-checklist of materials needed or important times and due dates to remember. Review this checklist regularly with the students.
6. Develop a personalized "What I Need to Remember" page with from three to five of the most important things you want the student to remember regularly. This sheet should then be prominently displayed on the inside cover of the student's binder.
7. Begin each class period with a review of the key points from your last class. End each class period with a student's participatory summary of that day's lesson.
8. Give students a blank or partially filled-in outline or web diagram at the beginning of class to help them organize their recording of information. (In a web diagram a student constructs a diagram showing the connection of related words to a key word.)
9. Help each student find and establish a method of notetaking that works best for him or her; for example, a web diagram or standard outline. Dated, preprinted sheets for the student to fill in the blanks accurately may be helpful.
10. Require students, with each change of activity, to clear their desks of all unnecessary material, books, and so forth that may distract them.
11. Set aside a regular time each week for students to clean out their desks and reorganize their binders.
12. Insist that the students carry a binder with delineated sections for each class and that each section have a pocket for homework assignments. Insist that one section of the folder be delegated for that day's homework assignments.
13. Give students, when using a workbook, only the pages they will need to do the present assignment. To start, the teacher's aide or another student may copy the instructions for the homework assignment for the student in order to ensure accurate recording. Gradually, this process should be delegated to the student.
14. Have the students periodically check the teacher's master list of all in-class and homework assignments previously given and the dates they are due.
15. Encourage students to read comprehension questions before beginning to read assignments. (The teacher, the textbook, or both provide comprehension questions for each story or chapter.) Help direct the student's finding answers from the textbook by writing the page number next to each question where the answer can be found.

16. Provide, at the top of practice work sheets, a model depicting sequenced steps to successful problem solving. Eliminate problems that do not fit the model.

17. Begin a writing assignment by having students record or orally give words or concepts they believe are relevant to the assigned topic. Younger students may benefit from drawing a picture of their ideas first. Older students may record their thoughts using a tape recorder so that they do not forget their ideas as they work through the actual writing process.

18. Provide a guide for structuring writing assignments. You might hand out a fill-in-the-blanks work sheet that requires the student to develop ideas or respond to specific topics; for example, main character, personality trait, or setting. Such a work sheet also provides an organizational format to facilitate the eventual construction of an essay.

Students' Attention Span

Difficulties   Difficulties in maintaining attention, commonly termed *inappropriate* or *short* attention span, may (1) be secondary to or associated with difficulties in processing specific or various types of information; (2) occur only in certain situations or environments (for example, a mismatch between learning and teaching styles or between teachers and students); (3) result from the effects of medications or a medical disorder; or (4) appear in students preoccupied with other concerns, thoughts, and feelings.

To be differentiated from a child's normal age-related behaviors and temperament, the characteristic behaviors listed below must occur **often** or **frequently**—either individually, in any combination, or in clusters. The student with a limited attention span may behave as follows:

1. Gives attention to the matter at hand or performs tasks inconsistently or unpredictably and often without explanation (The student is tuned-in on some occasions, tuned-out on others; does the same task very well sometimes and poorly at other times. A new skill is learned well one day and easily forgotten a few days later.)
2. Appears not to listen, daydreams, looks around, is "spacy" or stares, or notices things that no one else does
3. Becomes easily distracted or stops working on a task or starts another one, particularly during activities that are not interesting, highly stimulating, or enjoyable
4. Has difficulty concentrating on schoolwork, on tasks requiring sustained or prolonged attention, or on activities occurring in large groups
5. Demonstrates understanding of the main idea but misses important details
6. Has difficulty prioritizing the importance of material presented or overemphasizes or attends too much or too long to minor, less important, or irrelevant information
7. Has exaggerated inconsistencies in memory, generally for minor, unimportant, or useless details or for episodic, uneventful moments
8. Rushes through work, chores, or activities or gives up quickly
9. Becomes easily bored or restless, shifts excessively from one activity to another, is difficult to satisfy, wants things right away or thinks about what is coming next or later, and fails to finish things started or to stick to play activity
10. Appears not to plan or organize before taking action or starting to work
11. Acts or speaks out quickly and carelessly and without thinking about consequences
12. Blurts out answers impulsively, calls out in class, interrupts conversations or presentations with comments possibly having little or no connection with what is being said or done, and has difficulty awaiting a turn in group activities or games
13. Acts as if driven by a motor, has too much energy, and is always on the go (His or her body is in motion much of time, even during sleep.)
14. Has difficulty sitting still or remaining in his or her seat and fidgets excessively
15. Has variable, unpredictable behavior; makes trouble; stirs things up without meaning to get into trouble; and annoys or bothers others
16. Has difficulty realizing that he or she is disturbing others or understanding why he or she has trouble in getting along with peers
17. Has problems with recognizing own (or others') mistakes, learning from experience, or improving conduct after being disciplined or corrected

Students' Attention Span

Strategies In addition to the accommodations suggested in the section titled "Organizational Skills," students who have suspected attentional problems may need some other modifications in their learning environment. Issues of classroom management emerge as a primary consideration. Some behavioral-based strategies are suggested as follows:

1. Observe children's behavior critically to identify particular types of tasks, activities, or times of day when behavior unrelated to the learning task is prevalent or subsides. Recording these observations will help.

2. Prepare students well in advance for any changes in their otherwise consistent and predictable daily classroom routine to eliminate surprises whenever possible. Remind and reassure the students often.

3. Arrange classroom activities to shorten the teacher's presentation time and independent work periods. Include both kinds of activities during the class period to provide respite.

4. Develop activities that enable students to get out of their seats. Short periods of physical activity may alleviate restlessness and help to reduce the onset of distracting behaviors.

5. Provide a screened-off carrel or stand-up desk for independent work times or allow students to move to a quiet area in the room.

6. Establish a secret signal with the student (for example, a pat on the shoulder) to indicate that you believe that the student is off-task. The signal should gradually change from a physical touch to a signal given in proximity and, finally, to a subtle cue given from the regular teaching position.

7. Encourage the students to stop by your desk on their way out of class if they think they might have missed something important during the lesson. Help students to identify specifically what part of the instructions in the lesson they missed. This behavior indicates greater self-awareness and monitoring of attention. Avoid blaming or disciplining students during the discussion.

8. Clearly state your expectations for students' behavior and establish corresponding consequences for specific violations.

9. Develop a reward-based contract system that also contains clearly understood progressive consequences for targeted misbehaviors.

10. Consider the use of tangible reward systems or behavioral charts or both that focus on two or three of the child's most distracting behaviors. Reward students for "doing" correct or desired behaviors rather than emphasizing "not doing."

11. Take the minimum time necessary if time-out from an activity is required. Provide incentives for the student to rejoin the class.

12. Consider playing soft background music during independent work activities.

Difficulties with and Strategies for Demonstrating Performance

The following are areas in which students may have problems with demonstrating performance: verbal expression, handwriting and copying, spelling (encoding), written expression, mathematical computation, retention and retrieval of material presented, reduced productivity, and taking tests. Difficulties students may have in each of these areas are listed, followed by strategies to help them. These pages may be removed from this publication to facilitate their use for discussion.

Verbal Expression

Difficulties Students who have difficulties with verbal expression cannot easily convey their messages orally. This section deals with children who have trouble formulating what they want to say and then saying it. These students may behave as follows:

1. Are reticent to volunteer or participate in class discussions. May be shy with peers or adults or both.
2. Have difficulty responding instantly to oral questions.
3. Answer questions with short, clipped responses or provide nonelaborative responses.
4. Talk around subjects using colloquial rather than precise terms.
5. Have difficulty explaining themselves clearly and coherently.
6. Display poor mechanics of speech (for example, fluency, sentence structure, or finding words) or show subtle indicators of stuttering or stammering.
7. Have difficulty finding or retrieving the right word, as demonstrated by repetitions, reformulations, substitutions, delays, empty words, insertions, or the "tip-of-the-tongue" phenomenon.

Verbal Expression

General strategies for facilitating student's verbal expression are listed as follows:

1. Ask students questions when you know they will answer correctly rather than pose a question to assess their attentiveness.
2. Ask students having difficulty in answering a question with multiple components to provide an initial response or to give only one component.
3. Ask high-risk students questions requiring short verbal responses when the class is participating in a public forum.
4. Devise a clear and attainable structure for open-ended questions. For example, say, "Give me one way in which meteors and comets are alike" rather than say, "Tell me how comets and meteors are alike."
5. Allow students extra time to prepare their responses. Subtle time-buying strategies, such as posing a question, writing it on the board, and then erasing the board, will help students find and organize their words.
6. Provide "processing" and "retrieving" (word-finding) time for questions posed orally.
7. Give students who are having difficulty coming up with a word a cue for the initial sound or meaning of the word; for example, ask, "Who discovered electricity? His last name begins with an *F* sound."
8. Establish small discussion groups that address specifically designated questions and issues. This approach will enable the students to interact in a smaller, less demanding setting.
9. Designate a specific passage that you want students to read aloud; then give them silent preparation time. Select the passage that gives students the greatest chance of success. Shorten the amount to be read if necessary.
10. Allow students to prepare a script beforehand. To facilitate actual delivery, create a forum such as a puppet show for younger students or a radio talk show setting for older students.
11. Encourage students to make charts, diagrams, or illustrations to supplement oral reports. Model for them how to use these media to augment their presentations effectively.

Handwriting and Copying

Difficulties   Students who have difficulties with handwriting and copying often have trouble writing legibly or fast enough or both to keep up with notetaking, copying assignments, and answering essay questions. Doing homework that requires copying and writing is also difficult. These students are usually experiencing a neurological processing difficulty and are not intentionally being sloppy or careless. Rather, an underlying problem with integrating from visual to motor skills constricts the students' ability to perform writing or copying tasks or both efficiently.

Students who experience difficulty with handwriting and copying display the following characteristic behaviors:

1. They chronically demonstrate poor handwriting.
2. They hold their wrists, body, and paper in odd positions. Students may change their grip often or hold a pencil inappropriately or both. They may write with too much or too little pressure. Their fingers appear cramped on the writing tool.
3. They erase or cross out material excessively on paper and on the chalkboard.
4. They may have difficulty learning cursive forms and prefer printing over cursive writing. The quality of their printing and cursive writing differs significantly. They may be unable to read the teacher's cursive handwriting.
5. They do not form letters or letter connections in cursive writing automatically because they cannot recall the sequence of movements needed. They may display confusion between cursive letters such as *f* and *b, m* and *n*, and *w* and *u*.
6. They write in a mixture of upper-case and lower-case letters or a mixture of printed and cursive letters or both, or write them in irregular sizes and shapes.
7. They do not complete cursive letters, such as *i, j, t* and *x*.
8. They copy slowly and inefficiently with slow, labored handwriting.
9. They may draw excellently but find writing and copying arduous and difficult.
10. They may display difficulties with fine-motor skills when they manipulate small objects or tools, or they may be talented in these areas. This type of fine-motor skill does not necessarily transfer to handwriting skill.
11. They lose interest in or become easily fatigued during writing and copying tasks. Students' handwriting deteriorates as the activity progresses. Homework assignments that require copying and writing are often very difficult for the students to complete within reasonable time frames.
12. They have difficulty keeping up with copying, especially when the material is shown from a distance; for example, copying from a blackboard.
13. They may have difficulty with spatial organization when writing or copying. The students' letters, words, and numbers may go uphill or downhill or be cramped too close together or too far apart. Sometimes the students' letters or numbers may appear distorted or rotated.

Students who experience many of the classroom behaviors listed previously may be dysgraphic (handwriting and copying are not automatic functions). This condition should be understood by the student, teacher, and parent.

Handwriting and Copying

Strategies   The following general strategies are beneficial for the student who experiences difficulties with handwriting tasks:

1. Provide direct instruction in forming and connecting cursive letters, an activity that can be helpful. *Direct instruction* does not mean handing a student a ditto sheet of letter forms to be copied, nor does it mean increasing the number of copying tasks as a way to solve handwriting problems. Direct instruction in cursive handwriting involves a comprehensive overview of (1) spatial orientation on lined paper (the difference between letters that require one space *[a]* and two spaces *[d]*); (2) beginning, medial, and ending positions of letters (letters that begin on the bottom line *[i]* versus letters that begin at a "two o'clock position" *[c]* and letters that end on the last line *[e]* versus letters that end below the last line *[y]*); (3) analysis of letters that share beginning strokes, such as *l, h, b, f,* and so forth; and (4) analysis of how various letters are connected one to the other.

2. Keep ongoing dated samples showing the development of a child's writing if direct instruction in letter formation is offered. From these samples realistic evaluations of the child's progress can be made, and specific problems in the child's written work can be further analyzed.

3. Modify in-class writing assignments to include activities like fill-in-the-blanks, circle-the-answer, or short-answer sentence writing.

4. Require students whose work chronically shows messy erasures, excessive corrections, lack of neatness, and poor organization and students with significant writing disorders to use a pencil and skip lines when they write their first drafts and final versions of assignments.

5. Encourage the use of writing instruments that leave erasable marks and erasers that do not tear the paper.

6. Provide writing activities in groups so that the student can be paired or grouped with students who write legibly.

7. Encourage and support development of keyboarding and word processing computer skills. Accept computer-generated materials. A student lacking skills in handwriting and copying should not be asked to recopy in ink or pencil a paper written on a typewriter or a word processor.

8. Accept dictated material for homework assignments while such a student is learning keyboarding skills. Have parents write *dictated* across the top of the paper and instruct them not to reword the student's work.

9. Grade creative-writing assignments for content rather than for mechanics. Students lacking skills in copying and handwriting need successful writing experiences unmarred by technical difficulties. Such students are at risk for giving up if they are always graded down for a processing issue not within their control.

General strategies for facilitating students' copying skills are listed as follows:

1. Minimize the quantity of copying work required for a student to complete an assignment.
2. Pause periodically during a presentation to allow for questions and enable students to catch up with copying their notes.
3. Give students note sheets so that copying can be done from a near point (from a desk or a table) if copying is part of a lesson activity that involves acquiring new concepts.
4. Use a copying machine to enlarge labeling or fill-in-the-blanks spaces on prepublished handouts.
5. Give a student with legible handwriting some carbon paper or carbonless lined paper to use when assignments are being copied from the board. A clear and accurate copy is then given to the student having difficulty in copying the material. Minimize the amount of writing a child has to do while taking notes by providing a "fill-in-the-blanks outline" or a web diagram for class presentation.
6. Avoid teaching through copying tasks. (For instance, requiring students having difficulty in copying to copy spelling words multiple times and then write detailed sentences exemplifies a significant processing issue for those students.)
7. Encourage students, if possible, to use a lap-top computer or word processor for extended writing assignments as a way to enhance productivity.
8. Consider giving oral tests.
9. Note that students with developmental dysgraphia (nonautomatic handwriting and copying abilities) may also have specific learning disabilities, such as dyslexia, attention deficit disorder (ADD), attention deficit hyperactivity disorder (ADHD), or a coexistence of these conditions. If such a student is having difficulty reading, spelling, and staying focused during a writing task, along with having handwriting difficulties, a reduced homework load should be implemented; and extended time should be provided for test taking, especially when the test consists of significant writing tasks.

Spelling (Encoding)

Difficulties   Children who are having difficulty in learning and applying spelling (encoding) skills often display the following behaviors:

1. Appear to resist doing written work.
2. Submit scant writing samples with sentences that contain few words.
3. Have a writing vocabulary that seems diminished compared to their speaking vocabulary and overall grasp of concepts.
4. Show an increase in the number of spelling errors as a writing activity progresses.
5. Receive passing grades on spelling tests but spell poorly or erratically or both when writing.
6. Misspell words even when copying.
7. Appear unable to use a dictionary.
8. May continually misspell sight words (*thay* for *they, wen* for *when, bol* for *ball*) in spite of extensive practice.
9. May make transpositions (*gril* for *girl, no* for *on, own* for *won*), reversals (*ded* for *bed, dlack* for *black, qen* for *pen*), and inversions (*may* for *way, wnst* for *must, waut* for *want,* and *we* for *me*).
10. May display difficulty in learning homophones, such as *there, their,* and *they're,* in spite of extensive practice.
11. May display bizarre spelling errors in which the letters do not represent the sounds of the word being spelled (*sr* for *us, dool* for *ball, zt* for *fast*).

Spelling errors may indicate that a student has the following problems or confusions:

1. Difficulty in discriminating individual sounds within words
2. Difficulty in perceiving words as units of letters or sounds or both that can be broken apart or put together
3. Problems with hearing sounds in their correct sequence within words
4. Inability to remember the visual appearance of the words (*dorp* for *drop, dessert* for *desert, thay* for *they, wun* for *won,* and *wont* for *want*)
5. Problems with spelling according to the approximate sound of the word (*enuf* for *enough, kat* for *cat*)
6. Lack of knowledge of the structure and logic of written language (*dropt* for *dropped, nacher* for *nature*)
7. Lack of knowledge of the relationships between letters and sounds (*baf* for *book*)
8. Difficulty in learning sound and symbol relationships for vowels (*langthy* for *lengthy, Septimber* for *September, difficalt* for *difficult,* and *spouled* for *spoiled*)

Children who display noticeable difficulty in acquiring knowledge of the relationship between sounds and symbols are at risk for dyslexia. Difficulties with spelling are often an indicator of specific learning disabilities such as dyslexia.

Spelling (Encoding)

Strategies   Children experiencing spelling difficulties may not learn the structure of the language through immersion or by inference. Research studies indicate that these children require direct instruction to gain these skills. The following general strategies are listed to provide classroom support for students experiencing spelling difficulties:

1. Consider implementing a reading and spelling program that emphasizes:
   a. Providing simultaneous, multisensory language-based instruction
   b. Providing direct instruction in the logic and structure of language (Teach single-letter sound and symbol relationships as well as vowel and consonant blends, rules of syllabication, roots and affixes, parts of speech, and punctuation. Teach and reinforce high-probability rules for spelling. Do not teach confusing principles side by side. For example, many children become confused about spelling words with the short sound of *i* versus the short sound of *e*. Teach one of these two sounds extensively, not together.)
   c. Combining phonics with whole-language instruction
   d. Teaching correspondences between sounds and symbols and symbols and sounds
   e. Presenting skills in a logical sequence, beginning with the simplest, most frequently needed skills and advancing to less frequently encountered, more complex principles

2. Foster independent use of the previously listed instructional methods and learned skills by building strategies and by teaching the principles, often overlapping, that govern decoding and spelling and by promoting the use of interesting, meaningful, and relevant material early in the process of learning to read.

3. Display the phonetic symbols of new vocabulary and difficult words beside their spelling equivalent.

4. Grade the content of written materials instead of the mechanics. While a student is learning the structure of language or how to use tools and strategies, such as a computer with a spell checker or a calculator-type device programmed for spelling, the student will make multiple spelling errors. Continually giving low grades for spelling errors will frustrate the student unnecessarily and not appropriately reward the student's efforts to write.

5. Have students underline their words that they believe are misspelled. The teacher automatically corrects a student's underlined words before the final draft is produced. Allow students to use a portable spell checker in class.

6. Encourage children with persistent deficits in handwriting and spelling skills to seek directed instruction in computer use and keyboarding skills.

7. Understand that children with persistent difficulties in developing spelling skills do not seem to benefit from typical rote instruction of spelling. Students (and frequently their parents as well) may spend many hours each week on lists of spelling words, with little or no improvement in the students' ability to spell. Try substituting spelling lists that reinforce specific phonetic concepts being covered during direct instruction. Often five to ten words per list is sufficient.

Written Expression

Through written expression students are ultimately expected to convey their ideas and degree of understanding about topics presented. For students with learning problems, written expression is likely to be the language area in which they demonstrate the greatest deficit in their skills. Students may have the following problems:

1. They have difficulty writing answers correctly on paper but give correct answers when asked to respond orally.
2. Their written vocabulary is more simplistic than their speaking vocabulary.
3. Their poor knowledge of writing mechanics, such as punctuation and capitalization, obscures the clarity of their written assignments.
4. Their written content, although rich in ideas, may be poorly organized or lack coherence.
5. They write incomplete or run-on sentences or both as well as misspell frequently.
6. They achieve better test results on objective, fill-in-the-blanks, match-up, or short-answer tests than on essay tests or extended writing assignments.
7. They have a poor record for completing or handing in extended writing assignments.

Written Expression

Strategies   General strategies for facilitating students' skills in written expression are listed as follows:

1. Make specific comments about written work. Rather than generalizing about poor spelling, explain and demonstrate the rules on which the student makes chronic errors. Then require the student to proofread for only that particular skill.

2. Try not to write comments that reflect value judgments about the child's effort or the quality of the presentation. Note that handwriting is a fine motor skill and writing, a cognitive skill. Provide opportunities for students to develop and use word-processing skills (with appropriate word-processing programs) to encourage writing. Although formal keyboarding instruction, particularly for older students, would enhance their skills, the instruction is not a necessary prerequisite for using the keyboard to respond. Younger children benefit most from ongoing practice of word-processing skills in the classroom, developing keyboarding skills by using the equipment. Their skills can be refined later.

3. Give students some class time to work on written assignments so that the teacher may observe students firsthand and, if necessary, assist them with specific difficulties in preparing a writing assignment.

4. Give students two grades for written assignments: one for knowledge of content or creativity and one for sentence mechanics.

5. Create concept cards with models that emphasize rules, generalizations, and mechanics necessary for accurate writing. Color-coding and underlining a key part are helpful. Use concept cards regularly for class review before and during writing assignments.

6. Provide students with a proofreading checklist that clearly delineates which mechanical, organizational, and spelling skills will be evaluated for a particular assignment. Limit the number of mechanical skills to those that most affect the readability of the assignment. Emphasize the application of the simplest and most frequently used skills in grammar and mechanics.

7. Provide students, at the beginning of class, with a fill-in-the-blanks outline of an upcoming lecture. Provide visual cues when you are emphasizing a point that needs to be recorded on an outline.

8. Provide students, at the beginning of class, with written questions you will answer during the presentation. Supplement the questions with collaborative discovery learning activities as part of the assignment.

9. Consider allowing students to answer questions that best reflect the knowledge that you want them to have about a particular topic. Assign a reduced number of questions to be answered.

10. Ask students to draw a picture or diagram that addresses the assigned topic before they begin a writing assignment. This activity will help focus their thoughts and ideas.

11. Have students record their story, expository responses, or narrative, using a tape recorder so that essential thoughts and ideas may be preserved throughout the writing process.

12. Use teacher-initiated story starters or group round-robin writing activities.

13. Allow students to exchange and edit drafts before they hand them in. Pair a high-risk student with a proficient writer to minimize editing requirements and enable the student to observe and critique high-quality writing.

14. Allow students to do creative writing assignments in pairs. Form teams so that a student having difficulty with writing is paired with a student with strong writing skills.

15. Encourage students to use diagrams, charts, graphs, or illustrations to supplement written work.

16. Shorten the length of writing assignments without reducing expectations for the quality of the content. For short-answer assignments you might ask students to write phrases at first rather than sentences. Shorten essays from five to three paragraphs and gradually increase the length as the students show mastery.

17. Allow students periodically to do taped or live oral reports. This activity is particularly useful if the demonstration of newly acquired content knowledge is emphasized. You may still require an outline or a written summary.

Mathematical Computation

Some children understand the number system and can show that they know how to solve mathematical problems, yet their answers are incorrect. For those children the process of calculating numbers is frustrating. Children for whom mathematical computation is difficult have the following problems:

1. They have trouble remembering basic facts, details, and procedures. Their retention of mathematical knowledge is inconsistent or inaccurate or may worsen toward the end of an assignment or test.
2. They have trouble recalling details, placing numbers in the correct column, noticing changes or differences in the sign to be used, or determining the location of the decimal point.
3. They have difficulty remembering the sequence of steps in calculations.
4. They have difficulty recalling facts, details, and procedures quickly, precisely, and effortlessly or manipulating and remembering them while they solve the problem.
5. They can explain or demonstrate a solution to a problem but frequently make mistakes or have difficulty carrying out the process on paper.

Mathematical Computation

General strategies for facilitating students' skills in mathematical computation are listed as follows:

1. Use manipulatives whenever possible. At first, give students some free time to explore the materials. This activity will help students to discover many patterns and relationships. Students should then be guided toward discovery of specific concepts. To help students make these discoveries, ask directed questions and have students explore the concepts. Finally, relate the work with the manipulatives directly to tasks requiring paper, pencil, and a calculator. Allow students to use the manipulatives for as long as the students need them.

2. Accentuate the use of games and activities that simulate mathematical problems related to students' interests, needs, and realities.

3. Allow and encourage students to use calculators for computations on tests, classroom work, and homework assignments.

4. Modify the number of arithmetic problems by blocking out alternate rows of problems in a textbook or on a work sheet or by assigning only odd-numbered or even-numbered problems. This reduced work load allows for the extra processing time needed and limits copying, an arduous task for the student with developmental dysgraphia.

5. Eliminate copying from the board for students who display difficulty with copying tasks and handwriting. Give these students a printed copy of the problems or give a student with good handwriting some carbon paper or carbonless lined paper on which to make a legible copy for the designated student. When problems are to be copied from a far point (from the board), provide students with a sheet of problems that they can copy from a near point (at their desk). Because near-point copying tasks may be quite difficult for certain students, allow them to work on copies of the problems that are xeroxed or copied by another student.

6. Encourage students who display problems with number alignment, transpositions, and reversals to use graph paper to ensure organization of numbers within columns. The size of the grids on the graph paper should allow for comfort of copying and visual clarity.

7. Give students who display problems with number alignment, transpositions, and reversals some large, plain paper for computation. Have them fold it into desired fourths, eighths, and sixteenths to define and confine the working space. Have students turn a sheet of lined paper so that the lines are vertical and ask them to set up their mathematical problems so that they write only one number (digit) between the lines.

8. Allow students who display difficulty recognizing and changing signs to color-code the signs, because students benefit from this activity. Allow the students to choose different colored highlighters to color each operation. (For example, red might be chosen for subtraction [–] and green for addition [+]. Encourage the students to color work sheets and problems, using the appropriate colors to highlight all signs of operation before they begin to calculate.

9. Teach students who display difficulties with word problems the key vocabulary that identifies which mode of arithmetic computation is indicated.
10. Encourage students who display difficulties with word problems to use manipulatives and to create diagrams or pictures or both to aid in translating words into mathematical operations.
11. Provide a reader, if necessary, for students who may continue to have difficulty with word problems even though adaptations have been provided.
12. Provide extended time on tests and quizzes for students who display difficulties in mathematical computation, requiring extra time to process mathematical information. This adaptation is important for these students. If providing extended time is not feasible, the students should be graded only on the problems that they have completed during the testing period.
13. Encourage students who display mechanical errors to use scratch paper and enlarge their numbers. Also teach them self-checking methods and encourage them to recheck their work, allowing ample time.
14. Use a copy machine to enlarge the size of print or numbers so that the material on the page does not appear tiny and crowded.
15. Facilitate and encourage the use of computer-assisted instruction with software programs that focus on mathematical calculations. Programs available include activities in drill and practice with high-interest games and tutorials. Software programs with positive feedback, remediation, and recordkeeping are desirable.

Retention and Retrieval of Material Presented

Difficulties   Some students apparently have the answer on the tip of their tongue but cannot produce the answer. These students have difficulties with memory and recall. Students for whom retention and retrieval of material are difficult have the following problems:

1. They may not process information adequately or sufficiently, often because of poor selective attention.
2. They lack effective strategies for grouping incoming information into smaller useful units.
3. They have poor immediate or short-term memory and trouble retaining information in their short-term memory while they process other related information.
4. They have weak long-term memory for facts, details, procedures, skills, methods, and events in their lives.
5. They do not recall information quickly, accurately, or easily.
6. They can memorize and use material in one context or situation but cannot recall or use the same information in another.

Retention and Retrieval of Material Presented

Teachers must frequently repeat and review previously learned skills and concepts during classes in which new material is being introduced. Students should be allowed to discuss or do exercises that require them to recall what has been learned previously so that it, in fact, will become the foundation on which to build new learning. General strategies for facilitating students' retention and retrieval of material are listed as follows:

1. Begin each class by briefly summarizing orally or in writing the key concepts covered in the previous class. Highlight specific concepts and information you want students to retain for examinations.
2. At the end of class, provide handouts of key questions for the next day's lesson.
3. Provide or post a list of key terms you emphasized during a preceding unit when you are evaluating students' acquisition of concepts. You may then expect students to use the terms appropriately in written exercises.
4. Develop simple mnemonic devices to help students associate new vocabulary and concepts with familiar material.
5. Encourage subvocalization to help children respond to material just read. To provide for that need while a test is being given may require allowing the student to take a test in a separate room to avoid distracting others.
6. Teach students about the format and organization of textbooks so that they know where to look for various types of information and resources.
7. Use strategies to buy time when you are calling on students during a discussion. For example, if you want the class to "Give five reasons for ____," pose the question, erase the board while pausing (to make room for new responses), and call on the special student early.
8. Try to determine whether difficulties in recall stem from poor understanding, poor attention, distraction, mental or physical fatigue, or inadequate processing of information. Request information from the school psychologist if necessary.
9. Develop activities in which students can work in pairs; for example, assignments that allow students to combine a writing activity with drawing diagrams.
10. Teach the student effective strategies to reduce the amount of incoming information; for example, breaking information into meaningful chunks, repeating information silently or aloud, developing memory strategies to rehearse information, finding associations, or labeling information.
11. Teach strategies for comparing and associating new and old information. Examples are organizing information in particular sequences, categories, or classifications; visualizing or verbalizing information or both; and memorizing through generalizations, principles, or rules.
12. Place facts in context when you are teaching them and show how they are related.
13. Help establish strong, meaningful links between seemingly separate pieces of information.
14. Develop strong connections between current and previous learning experiences.
15. Provide learning objectives at the beginning of a unit of study and summarize them at the end of the unit.

Reduced Productivity

Despite goals, negotiations, or reward or punishment, students for whom reduced productivity is a problem seem to get less done than their classmates. This section focuses on students who simply process information more slowly than others and consequently complete less work within a comparable time frame. Students who work more slowly than their classmates may have the following problems:

1. Their written assignments are shorter in length than those of fellow classmates.
2. They do not complete in-class independent assignments even though their attention seems to be focused on their work.
3. They are considerably slower in completing timed drill exercises than other classmates are.
4. They complain of writer's cramp or discomfort in writing because they grip their pencil awkwardly or too tightly or apply too much pressure on the paper.
5. Their approach to problem solving is disorganized, unplanned, rigid, or impulsive.
6. They think too long when they are given tasks that require one to rank multiple possible responses according to their importance.
7. They become fatigued more quickly during presentations or activities that require rapid integration, retrieval, and responses to complex material or difficult concepts or both.

Reduced Productivity

Strategies Students' reduced productivity is caused primarily by problems with processing, retrieval, or retention of information. Children with these learning problems cannot be made to work faster without significantly compromising the accuracy or legibility of their work. General strategies for facilitating students' problems related to reduced productivity are listed as follows:

1. Alleviate students' anxiety about performing a task quickly. This approach will enable them to perform near their potential. Make accommodations for time.
2. Observe carefully whether distraction of the student may be the source of his or her reduced productivity. If so, then refer to the strategies in the section titled "Students' Attention Span."
3. Allow students to provide essays or answers that are short but still demonstrate knowledge comparable to that of other students in the class.
4. Provide the student with a study partner who does not exhibit any learning difficulties. The study partner can take notes using carbon paper when important information is to be presented in fine points (in great detail) and when notetaking must be done in conjunction with listening tasks. You may also photocopy notes for a special student.
5. Provide a blank web diagram or flowchart format for the student to fill in during class discussion or to help structure ideas for notetaking and recording.
6. Have the material in a textbook tape-recorded if the quantity of reading material is an issue so that the child can follow the material while getting the needed verbal input. Tape-recording of textbooks is an excellent use of classroom volunteers, aides, or peer tutors.
7. Provide students with a computer and appropriate programs to facilitate productivity and build strategies, especially in writing.

Taking Tests

The student with problems in taking tests often has trouble in showing what he or she knows when faced with the task of performing independently. This situation is particularly true for tests that require writing sentences or reading paragraphs. The student may do the following:

1. Delay looking at the test paper.
2. Ignore key elements of the instructions.
3. Lose his or her place when switching from a test booklet to an answer sheet.
4. Make errors in identifying the question or item to which he or she is responding.
5. Make corrections and erasures even though they are not allowed.
6. Make excuses for not taking the test or plead sickness.
7. Spend an inordinate amount of time on one or a few items and not finish the remainder.
8. Miss the point of an essay question and write about a minor detail.
9. Make wild or random guesses.
10. Mark answers in a pattern.
11. Ask leading questions out loud or attempt to get help during testing.
12. Give up before starting to answer the items and complete no part of the test.
13. Have difficulty shading in ovals on test sheets.

Taking Tests

Strategies for facilitating classroom testing with teacher-made tests and with standardized tests will be presented in this section.

Teacher-made tests. General strategies for facilitating the use of teacher-made tests are listed as follows:

1. Conduct a review session before the test. Distribute a study guide that highlights key terms and concepts to be addressed.
2. Give frequent quizzes to reduce the quantity of material covered on a test and enable students to recover from a poor grade.
3. Give credit for class participation, project completion, in-class work, and work samples, when possible, so that a student's grade does not depend entirely on test results.
4. Administer untimed tests or at least allow students more time (from 1.5 to 2 times more) to complete tests.
5. Adhere closely to stated behavioral objectives of the lesson or assignment when you design assessment measures. Avoid asking students to perform on the test differently from the way they prepared for it; for example, giving a student a timed paper-and-pencil test of mathematics facts after he or she was asked to study with flash cards.
6. At the top of examination sheets, list the vocabulary words to be used on fill-in-the-blanks exercises. Limit the number of fill-in-the-blanks, match-ups, and multiple-choice questions so that the quantity of test items is not overwhelming.
7. Consider administering tests in special circumstances; for example, one-on-one, orally, in a special room, or at a special time. Make arrangements ahead of time with the student because the accommodations are made to reduce test anxiety, not increase it.
8. Have students demonstrate their knowledge in ways other than paper-and-pencil tests.

If the student has problems with verbal expression, consider incorporating the following activities:

1. Providing oral interview questions ahead of time so that the student can prepare responses
2. Assigning students to prepare tape recordings of their answers or conducting one-on-one interviews rather than requiring students to present their responses publicly
3. Arranging for alternative modes of response, such as preparing a written or demonstration activity
4. Allowing students to use illustrations, diagrams, and charts to supplement oral presentations
5. Allowing students to submit written scripts of their responses that can be weighted with their verbal performance

If the student has problems with written expression, consider incorporating the following activities:

1. Using testing formats that reduce the amount of writing required (Use short-answer, multiple-choice, match-up, and fill-in-the-blanks options.)
2. Allowing students to write on the test sheet rather than copy answers on a separate page (This activity reduces the possibility of circling right answers on the wrong line.)
3. Permitting the student to use his or her preferred mode of handwriting
4. Providing separate evaluations for the content and for spelling and mechanics of language (Be sure to emphasize the grade for knowledge of content. Once the test has been graded for the student's knowledge of content, offer the student the opportunity to correct mistakes in mechanics and spelling before the final test grade is recorded.)
5. Allowing students to demonstrate knowledge through supplementary use of web diagrams, captioned illustrations, charts, and graphs
6. Offering students the option of providing answers to the essay portion of major examinations during conferences with teachers or with tape recorders (The student can then complete the remaining short-answer sections by hand.)
7. Administering open-note, open-book, or take-home examinations
8. Presenting the examination on an off-white sheet of paper to facilitate the comfort of sustained vision
9. Using oral, acting, or visual art activities may be more reliable ways to measure acquisition of skills or concepts than the use of conventional methods

Standardized tests. General strategies for facilitating the use of standardized tests are listed as follows:

1. Arrange for students to take tests in smaller groups or with a special administrator as a way to reduce anxiety.
2. Give a practice test the day before a test is to be administered that simulates the type of questions and responses that will be required on the formal test. This activity will help orient the student to the test format and help to reduce anxiety.
3. Be sure that the student has answered the sample questions accurately and in the right place.
4. Allow students to code words or underline perceived key points as they read in the test booklet.
5. Allow students to use blocking instruments, such as blank index cards, to reduce stimulus on the visual field and to aid the students in keeping their place when reading.
6. Highlight even-numbered (or every fifth) question and answer in both the test booklet and answer sheet so that the student can self-monitor the matching of an item with its response number or oval.

CHAPTER III

Learning Disabilities and Related Disabilities

$\mathbf{T}$*he purpose of this chapter is to discuss briefly some of the related disabilities or conditions included under the legal definition of* specific learning disabilities. *The reader is given an overview of the variety of conditions and of some of the unique ways in which schools approach this area of disability.*

Background Information

In chapters I and II, the project members brought together the accommodations and strategies that can be applied in the general classroom and that the members have found helpful in their teaching experience. Some suggestions were made on how to select and implement these accommodations. The lists of difficulties and strategies were prepared for students with a broad spectrum of general learning difficulties and not related to objectives for a particular assessed disability or disorder.

In contrast to the material presented for the general classroom in chapters I and II, Chapter IV examines, in depth, the definition and procedures for assessment of a child's *specific learning disability* to determine whether it qualifies as a disability under the provisions of the Individuals with Disabilities Education Act (IDEA) and California state laws and regulations. Readers may wish to examine Chapter IV in relation to material from this chapter.

Specific Learning Disabilities

The concept of specific learning disabilities has come from the fields of medicine, psychology, psychiatry, neurology, education, and special education. Some practitioners look for causes of observed behaviors; others look at the effects of the behaviors. Regardless of the differing approaches to etiology, definition, and treatment of specific learning disabilities, the most common characteristic of such disabilities in children is that the children manifest an educationally significant discrepancy between their apparent capacity for learning and their actual level of functioning in the classroom. Another characteristic is that the children lack certain conditions; that is, their learning problems are not due to sensory deficits, motor impairment, mental retardation, or inadequate schooling. These two characteristics appear in the current definitions of *specific learning disabilities.*

Note: This chapter was developed after the project had been completed.

The *Code of Federal Regulations, Title 34,* Part 300.7(b)(10) [34 *CFR* 300.7] states that:

> "Specific learning disability" means a disorder in one or more of the basic psychological processes involved in understanding or in using language, spoken or written, that may manifest itself in an imperfect ability to listen, think, speak, read, write, spell, or to do mathematical calculations. The term includes such conditions as perceptual disabilities, brain injury, minimal brain dysfunction, dyslexia, and developmental aphasia. The term does not apply to children who have learning problems that are primarily the result of visual, hearing, or motor disabilities, of mental retardation, of emotional disturbance, or of environmental, cultural, or economic disadvantage.

This definition grew out of a broad area of study and research influenced by several disciplines and limited by very few measurable factors that define the existence of the condition. Over time educational processes have increasingly influenced the concept as special education sought ways to provide an appropriate education. The parent, student, and educators need to determine the conditions that the student may have in order to decide whether the student can continue to make progress in the general education classroom (most can); which modifications to the classroom procedures would benefit the student; which specialized instruction or technology might enhance the learning process; and whether (in occasional cases) the disability and behaviors can be dealt with more effectively through a different approach, especially when a learning disability is a component of a multiple disability, such as attention deficit, retardation, autism, or emotional disturbance.

A suspected learning disability must be carefully evaluated. When modifications tried by the classroom teacher and the support (including assistance with homework) provided by parents are unsuccessful, the various factors that contribute to a student's continuing problems will need to be assessed. The academic strengths and weaknesses of the student, especially how well the student processes language, must be determined. Assessing the context and circumstances in which the problems occur is also important to determine possible factors in the environment that contribute to or influence the learning process. The student's behaviors must be assessed as an indicator of how well the student is coping with school and of the effect of the disability on the student's self-esteem and motivation to achieve.

During the nineties a resurgence of interest in the definition of *specific learning disabilities* is occurring because (1) a strong belief has developed that mild to moderate learning disabilities are best managed in the general classroom through support delivered within the classroom; (2) growth in differentiated fields of study is resulting in new and technologically sophisticated research from which new concepts are emerging; for example, regarding the functioning of the brain and language learning disabilities; (3) concepts of cognitive behavior stress the individuality of the learning experience; and (4) ecological concepts (interaction between the individual and the environment) emphasize the school's responsibility for teaching strategies for coping and solving problems. These strategies are equally as important as academic instruction, if not more. Individuals need to understand and learn to cope with a learning disability.

Almost all students experience general problems in learning at some time. Chapters I and II present strategies to help these students in the general classroom. The term *specific learning disabilities*, however, includes a broad and diverse constellation of conditions too extensive to describe briefly in this chapter, and the conditions require careful assessment and evaluation. This chapter next examines some of the related conditions frequently seen as a specific set of behaviors included under the term *learning disabilities*.

Related Disabilities

The definition of *specific learning disability* in the *Code of Federal Regulations* contains this sentence: "The term includes such conditions as perceptual disabilities, brain injury, minimal brain dysfunction, dyslexia, and developmental aphasia" (34 *CFR* 300.7 [b][10]). Many other terms appear in the literature or in assessment reports, such as *dysgraphia, dyscalculia, apraxia,* and *attention deficits*. (See the Glossary for a description of these and related terms.)

The names are terms that have come from popular usage. *Dys* in medical terminology means "difficulty with or disorder of." *A* means "without or not"; that is, "a total lack of the capability." However, *aphasia* is preferred over *dysphasia,* while *dyslexia* is more widely used than *alexia;* and both commonly refer to the full range of the condition. On the other hand, *attention deficit* comes from ordinary descriptive terms. Three of these areas are discussed in this chapter: developmental aphasia, dyslexia, and attention deficit. Also discussed is one area that often accompanies a learning disability and can be thought of in the same context—students' behavior.

Developmental Aphasia

Developmental aphasia is a disorder in learning and using spoken or oral language. This condition is included as a learning disability, except that it is more often within the purview of the large and long-standing profession of language, speech, and hearing specialists. Aphasia is one of many speech and language disabilities that include problems with articulation, auditory skills, and voice. The discipline has professionals credentialed to provide special education services and who may also assist general classroom teachers in providing developmental language instruction. Special classes are provided for the more seriously disabled aphasic students and are taught by teachers from backgrounds in language, speech, and hearing or in learning disabilities, depending on each state's policies. Other professionals licensed by the state provide services in clinics, hospitals, or private practice.

Aphasia as a disability will not be discussed further in this document and was included to provide a perspective on the breadth of learning disabilities. In the larger context of students who have difficulty in learning from conventional instruction, students with aphasia have complex problems with learning language. Persons wishing to learn more about this disability should consult their local language, speech, and hearing specialist or special education director.

Dyslexia

Dyslexia is a disorder that results in difficulty in learning the written or symbol language skills of reading, writing, and spelling through conventional instruction. California has no official definition, but the Texas *Educational Code,* Section 21.924, defines *dyslexia* as follows:

1. *Dyslexia* means a disorder of constitutional origin manifested by a difficulty in learning to read, write, or spell, despite conventional instruction, adequate intelligence, and sociocultural opportunity.
2. *Related disorders* includes disorders similar to or related to dyslexia such as developmental auditory imperception, dysphasia, specific developmental dyslexia, developmental dysgraphia, and developmental spelling disability.

The World Federation of Neurology defines developmental dyslexia as follows (Critchley, 1968):

Specific Developmental Dyslexia: A disorder manifested by difficulty in learning to read despite conventional instruction, adequate intelligence, and sociocultural opportunity. It is dependent upon fundamental cognitive disabilities which are frequently of a constitutional origin.

Dyslexia: A disorder in children, who, despite conventional classroom experience, fail to attain the language skills of reading, writing, and spelling commensurate with their intellectual abilities.

The relatively extensive body of knowledge available on dyslexia is largely due to the early studies done by Samuel T. Orton, M.D., a neuropathologist and psychiatrist, whose articles were first published in 1925. One year after his death in 1948, a nonprofit, international organization, the Orton Dyslexia Society, was formed, which continues to provide community service. This society—composed of scientists, educators, doctors, speech and language pathologists, psychiatrists, neurologists, and of other professionals as well as of families and individuals who experience dyslexia—promotes effective teaching approaches and related clinical and educational intervention strategies for dyslexics of all ages. This organization also supports and encourages interdisciplinary study and research of dyslexia.

Substantial research studies of the brain have been and are being done at Harvard University, as well as at other research facilities, to understand dyslexia better. These studies clearly indicate that the architecture of the dyslexic brain differs significantly from that of the nondyslexic brain. Scientific studies continue to substantiate the opinion that the structure of the dyslexic brain frequently brings "gifts" or talents in visual-spatial, three-dimensional, or abstract reasoning or a combination of the three. The architecture of the dyslexic brain is also thought to be the causative factor underlying the extreme difficulty that dyslexics manifest in learning and applying written language skills (Galaburda, 1989, 78.)

Note: The material on dyslexia in this chapter was taken from a forthcoming book by Yana Livesay, "Dyslexia: At Last Some Answers." Yana Livesay, Dyslexia Treatment and Counseling Center, 940 Saratoga Ave., Suite 205, San Jose, CA 95129.

Characteristics of Dyslexia

As with any of the specific learning disabilities, a professional can determine whether a person has dyslexia from the presence of a *constellation* of characteristics. The same is true of medical and psychological disorders as well, because no single factor can determine a syndrome.

Children who have difficulty learning to read are not necessarily dyslexic. Reading difficulties can occur for a variety of reasons, and dyslexia is only one of many possibilities. Furthermore, all of the characteristics listed in connection with dyslexia do not necessarily have to be found in any one child. Rather, a preponderance of characteristics in specific patterns typical of dyslexia indicate its presence.

The lists of characteristics presented in this chapter are not meant to be used as diagnostic criteria. Instead, the characteristics listed in the sections that follow represent *informal* observations of behaviors commonly noted in dyslexic students. Diagnosis of dyslexia, and of any other specific learning disability, must be determined by a complete and thorough assessment administered by a trained professional. A psycholinguistic assessment that measures receptive and expressive oral and written language processes is used to identify dyslexia *formally* (Green, 1993). Extensive professional training and expertise are required in rendering this type of formal determination.

Nevertheless, the characteristics included in this chapter can be helpful for identifying children who are at risk for dyslexia and therefore require immediate assistance from teachers and parents through appropriate classroom accommodations and the use of tools, strategies, and interventions (direct instruction).

The following sections contain groupings of learning difficulties that dyslexic children frequently experience. The degrees of difficulty a child experiences will vary for each child, as will overall patterns of strengths and weaknesses that a child demonstrates. The differing degrees and patterns depend on the type and severity of the dyslexia, the coexistence of other specific learning disabilities, such as attention deficit disorder, or both.

Reading, Writing, and Spelling Skills

Children with dyslexia frequently have difficulties acquiring reading, writing, and spelling skills commensurate with their intellectual ability. The following three sections list the specific classroom behaviors observed in children experiencing these difficulties.

Difficulties with reading. Dyslexic children experiencing difficulties with reading may:

1. Have problems learning the letters of the alphabet or learning to write the alphabet in correct sequence or both.
2. Have problems learning or applying word attack skills or both.
3. Make reading errors that display reversals (*ded* for *bed, bog* for *dog*); transpositions (*was* for *saw, gril* for *girl, no* for *on, own* for *won*); or inversions (*may* for *way, we* for *me*).
4. Display problems in learning to read phonetically irregular sight words (*one, was, through*).
5. Omit, add, or misread small function or connecting words (*an, a, and, of, from, were, are*).
6. Read letters in the wrong order (*felt* for *left, act* for *cat, reserve* for *reverse, expect* for *except*).

7. Confuse the short vowels (*ledy* for *lady, beg* for *bag, lid* for *led*).
8. Misread initial consonants, reversing them (*dad* for *bad, dig* for *big*); inverting them (*put* for *but, pang* for *bang, dot* for *pot*); or inserting consonants that are visually similar (*hight* for *night, now* for *how*).
9. Misread words of similar visual appearance regardless of meaning, making gestalt replacements (*sunrise* for *surprise, house* for *horse, through* for *though, while* for *white, wanting* for *walking, single* for *signal*).
10. Substitute another word of similar meaning, making a semantic substitution (*wet* for *water, travel* for *journey, fast* for *speed, cry* for *weep*).
11. Omit prefixes, especially *non-* and *un-* (*sense* for *nonsense, happy* for *unhappy, done* for *undone*).
12. Omit or change suffixes (*need* for *needed, mineral* for *minerals, learns* for *learned, spent* for *spends*).
13. Lose concepts because of misreading or misunderstanding words that appear similar (*country-county, historical-hysterical*).
14. Avoid reading if possible and not read for pleasure.
15. Learn to read well enough to get by in elementary school only to encounter difficulty in junior high school.
16. Read at grade level but still not at a level commensurate with intelligence.
17. Read aloud with a choppy cadence and seem unable to observe punctuation or pauses or both.
18. Read very slowly.
19. Become visibly fatigued after spending only a short time reading.

Difficulties with writing. Dyslexic children experiencing difficulties with writing may:

1. Have adequate (or even superior) ability in oral expression but display poor or impoverished written expression.
2. Have poor use of syntax, prefixes, and suffixes.
3. Appear to resist written work.
4. Show numerous self-corrections on written work, often related to reversals, transpositions, inversions, or confusions about letter formations or spelling.
5. Have problems with learning parts of speech (grammar).
6. Chronically forget to punctuate and capitalize appropriately.
7. Display difficulty with acquisition of proofreading skills.
8. Miss many errors in written work, even when proofreading has been attempted.

Difficulties with spelling. Dyslexic children experiencing difficulties with spelling may:

1. Have significant difficulty in learning and applying phonological awareness.
2. Continually misspell sight words (*thay* for *they, wen* for *when, bol* for *ball*) in spite of extensive exposure and practice.
3. Misspell even when copying.
4. Display spelling errors of transposition (*gril* for *girl, own* for *won, hepl* for *help*); reversals (*dlack* for *black, qen* for *pen, ded* for *bed*); or inversions (*may* for *way, wnst* for *must, waut* for *want, we* for *me*).
5. Display bizarre spelling errors; that is, the letters used do not represent sounds in the word dictated (*sr* for *us, dool* for *ball, zt* for *fast, baf* for *book*).

6. Attempt to spell according to the approximate sound of the word (*c* for *see, enuf* for *enough, kat* for *cat*).
7. Have difficulty in learning vowel and vowel blend sound to symbol relationships (*langthy* for *lengthy, Septimber* for *September, difficalt* for *difficult, spouled* for *spoiled*).
8. Receive passing grades on weekly spelling tests (by memorizing the list of words) but spell poorly on writing assignments or the review test.
9. Display poor visual memory for the shape of words, especially for those that are phonetically irregular or that are exceptions to spelling rules (*wont* for *want, dessert* for *desert, thay* for *they, wun* for *won*).
10. Display a lack of knowledge regarding the structure and logic of written language (*dropt* for *dropped, nacher* for *nature*).

Other Classroom Skills

In addition to discrepancies between their skills in reading, writing, and spelling and their intellectual abilities, dyslexic children may also have difficulties with other classroom skills, including:

1. Penmanship
2. Directionality
3. Sequencing
4. Concepts of time
5. Spatial organization
6. Rote memorization

The following sections list the specific classroom behaviors observed in children experiencing difficulties in these areas.

Difficulties with producing neat and efficient penmanship. Dyslexic children experiencing difficulties with penmanship may:

1. Chronically demonstrate poor or illegible handwriting.
2. Exhibit slow, labored, or arduous processing of handwriting or copying tasks or both.
3. Grip a pencil in an unusual manner.
4. Erase or cross out material excessively on paper or chalkboard.
5. Produce handwriting that is distorted, rotated, poorly spaced, or inconsistent (both in forms and letter slant).
6. Often shake out the hand used for writing while performing a writing task and may complain of hand cramping.
7. Have difficulty in learning cursive letter forms.
8. Chronically forget to finish cursive letters, such as *i, j, t,* or *x.*
9. Chronically show confusion about similar letter forms, such as *f* and *b, m* and *n, w* and *u.*
10. Forget cursive capital letter forms for such letters as *S* and *L.*
11. Show noticeable resistance to writing or copying tasks.
12. Display difficulty in keeping up with copying from the chalkboard or taking notes in class or both.

13. Struggle to recall sequential movement patterns necessary for automatic letter formation.
14. Form letters and numbers from an unusual starting position.
15. Have difficulty in understanding where to write on a numbered page, workbook, or test form.

Difficulties with directionality. Dyslexic children experiencing difficulties with directionality may:

1. Reverse letters or numbers (*b* for *d, p* for *q*).
2. Transpose letters and numbers (*was* for *saw, bran* for *barn, 547* for *457*).
3. Invert letters and numbers (*p* for *b, q* for *d, 9* for *6, u* for *n*).
4. Be late in establishing preferred hand for writing (ambivalent dominance).
5. Write with one hand and play sports with another (cross-dominance).
6. Display confusion regarding how to begin and end letter or number forms.
7. Rotate letters, numbers, and other symbols (× for +).
8. Have difficulty in learning the language of directionality (left and right, up and down, under and over, before and after, ahead and behind, foreword and backward, east and west).
9. Have difficulty in learning that addition, subtraction, and multiplication problems are worked from right to left (as opposed to reading from left to right), whereas long division is worked from left to right.
10. Become confused about left-right directionality when working with positive and negative numbers, decimal manipulations, or all three numerical operations.
11. Confuse direction when carrying a digit in a mathematics problem.

Difficulties with sequencing. Sequencing refers to the order of steps to be completed in a process. Dyslexic children experiencing difficulties with sequencing may have difficulty:

1. Remembering the sequence of movements necessary to form letters or numbers
2. Memorizing the months of the year or days of the week in proper sequence
3. Remembering the sequence of procedures necessary to work a long-division problem
4. Learning tasks that require a specific sequencing of steps

Difficulties with learning concepts of time. Dyslexic children experiencing difficulties with learning concepts of time may:

1. Have difficulty in telling time (especially with an analog clock).
2. Have difficulty in learning temporal sequences or concepts or both, such as:
   a. Months of the year
   b. Days of the week
   c. Hours in a day
   d. Yesterday, today, and tomorrow
   e. Last week, next week, one year ago, and next year
3. Be chronically tardy to class.
4. Be chronically late handing in homework.
5. Omit dates on homework papers or often write the wrong dates.

6. Have difficulty in using an assignment calendar. For example, they may:
   a. Become confused about due dates (misunderstand where four weeks from today should be annotated).
   b. Seem unable to organize long-term assignments into smaller units.
   c. Not annotate enough information to record the complete or appropriate assignment.
   d. Appear overwhelmed by a week-at-a-glance format because of difficulties in anticipating time.
7. Have difficulty, when enrolled in middle school, in remembering the sequence and times of specific classes.

Difficulties with spatial organization. Dyslexic children experiencing difficulties with spatial organization may:

1. Have difficulty in getting books, other school materials, and complete homework assignments home.
2. Have inordinate difficulty in returning homework to the classroom because it has been lost in a book, backpack, or locker.
3. Chronically misplace materials for classroom use, including books, pencils, and handouts.
4. Have an unusually messy desk, locker, or room.
5. Have unusual difficulty in cleaning and organizing a desk, locker, or room.
6. Lose personal belongings, such as coats, sweaters, shoes, watches, or lunches.
7. Carry all books and materials in a backpack rather than use a locker for fear of inability to organize proper materials on a class-by-class basis.
8. Have difficulty in organizing study space in class, at home, or both.
9. Have difficulty in determining which school materials are necessary for a given assignment.

Difficulties in memorizing by rote. Dyslexic children experiencing difficulties in memorizing by rote may:

1. Have an excellent grasp of mathematical concepts but appear unable to memorize mathematical facts, such as multiplication times tables.
2. Be capable of understanding the underlying concepts or reasons for a historical event but seem unable to remember the names, dates, or places regarding the event.
3. Have difficulty in recalling the names of people, places, or things.

Dyslexia Plus Syndrome

More than one specific learning disability can coexist within a learning disabled child. When this condition occurs in a dyslexic child, it is called *dyslexia plus syndrome.* The combination of several specific learning disabilities can complicate significantly the child's overall profiles of strengths and weaknesses.

One of the most common entities that may coexist with dyslexia is attention deficit disorder (ADD), with or without the hyperactivity component. Statistics from scientific, medical, and educational researchers vary regarding the coexistence of these two learning disabilities. Children can have one disability without the other; but research studies suggest a probability of approximately 30 percent that dyslexia and attention deficit disorder can coexist (often termed comorbidity) (Goldstein and Goldstein, 1992, 8; Silver, n.d.) Therefore, if characteristics of dyslexia seem present in any given child, it is always wise to consider the characteristics of attention deficit disorder (ADD) or attention deficit hyperactivity disorder (ADHD) as well. The child who displays patterns of both of these learning disabilities will probably need more extensive interventions overall.

Over the past 12 years researchers have noted that some dyslexic children experience a light-sensitivity syndrome that makes them unusually sensitive to light, color, and contrast. This sensitivity can adversely affect one's perception of black print on a white page and is usually the most pronounced when reading takes place under fluorescent lighting. A research study by Margaret S. Livingstone and others, whose findings appear in "Physiological and Anatomical Evidence for a Magnocellular Defect in Developmental Dyslexia," is beginning to identify why this phenomenon may occur (Livingstone, and others, 1991, 7943–47). However, much remains to be learned and understood.

A population of dyslexic children also exists who experience significant difficulties with word retrieval. Many dyslexic children have more fully developed abilities in verbal expression in comparison to their often poorly developed abilities in written expression. Although at times most dyslexic children exhibit some problems with word retrieval when recalling the names of people, places, and things, these difficulties are frequently intermittent and not especially detrimental to the children's classroom performance. The combination in children of dyslexia and expressive language deficit disorder (also called *dysnomia* or *dysphasia*) significantly affects their school performance. These children not only have difficulty in expressing themselves in writing but also have much difficulty in expressing their well-developed thoughts, ideas, and feelings in words. These children's intellectual ability and academic motivation are often underestimated.

Summary

Dyslexic children display characteristic patterns of difficulties with language processing as well as characteristic strengths in other areas. Dyslexic children's unique patterns of learning can produce distinctive classroom behaviors that are observable by both teachers and parents. However, a formal diagnosis of dyslexia is determined through a psycholinguistic assessment administered and scored by a highly trained professional.

Dyslexic children manifest skills and preferences of learning styles in many areas of visual-spatial, three-dimensional activities (involving plastic construction blocks, art activities, video games, hands-on projects, science projects, or athletics); abstract reasoning (social nuances or interrelationship of concepts); mechanical abilities (how things work, fit together, or come apart); and practical knowledge in general (horse sense).

Dyslexic children often demonstrate a lack of natural talent in the development of reading, writing, or spelling skills; concepts of directionality; sequencing of tasks; and rote memorization of facts, figures, names, and dates. They may also have difficulty in forming neat and automatic penmanship, managing time, and developing concepts of spatial organization.

Scientific and medical research studies indicate that dyslexia is a manifestation of anatomical and functional differences in the central nervous system and that the origin of dyslexia is usually constitutional (hereditary). Disorders resulting from dyslexia can range from mild to very severe. Children with dyslexia may also have other specific learning disabilities. Therefore, the patterns of dyslexia will vary for each child. Some children will manifest most of the characteristics listed in this chapter; others will manifest many in one area and only a few or none in another. Because dyslexia is represented by a constellation of language processing difficulties, a child who exhibits only a few of the characteristics listed in this chapter is unlikely to be dyslexic.

A dyslexic child's neurological difficulty in acquiring and mastering sound to symbol relationships (symbol to sound for reading and sound to symbol for spelling) is probably the most significant underlying cause of the difficulties that this child experiences when learning to read and spell (Aaron, 1989, 125; Aaron and Baker, 1991, 38–41). Dyslexic children do not learn the phonological basis or structure of written language implicitly. Children with moderate to severe neurological syndromes of dyslexia will usually need specialized assistance in the form of direct instruction (Chall, 1987, 22; Slingerland, 1982, 30–35). Without this specialized assistance, the dyslexic child must rely heavily on compensatory strategies that are often insufficient and prevent the child from achieving academic success commensurate with his or her intellectual potential.

The dyslexic child who needs specialized assistance and does not receive appropriate interventions will, almost daily, experience more academic failures than successes. This situation quickly erodes a child's self-esteem and motivation to pursue academic subjects. These students may even be thought to have a *primary* psychological or behavioral barrier to learning. However, more commonly, they are expressing emotions or behaviors that are largely secondary to an innate neurological language processing disorder.

A dyslexic child will often require a combination of appropriate classroom adaptations and access to and training in the use of compensatory tools and strategies, along with appropriate direct teaching interventions. Teachers' and parents' understanding of the dyslexic child's unique patterns of strengths and weaknesses will protect and nurture the child's self-esteem while strategies and interventions are being implemented.

The reader is encouraged to review the material in Chapter II, which presents many strategies that can be used to help these students.

Attention Deficits

A student with attention deficits (attention deficit disorder [ADD] or attention deficit hyperactivity disorder [ADHD]) becomes inattentive, hyperactive, or impulsive or a combination of those behaviors, affecting his or her ability to learn. The area has been identified from research studies from several disciplines but primarily from neurological studies of the behavioral symptoms of the brain-injured, especially of servicemen following World War I and then more intensely in studies of children from rehabilitation research studies done after World War II.

The Glossary gives the current definition of *attention deficit disorder* and *attention deficit hyperactivity disorder* from the *Diagnostic and Statistical Manual of Mental Disorders (DSM) III-R,* published in 1987. The task force on *DSM IV* made major revisions in the definition in 1993; and, most likely, that draft will be adopted. It has been included here to illustrate the changes and show the manner of identifying at least six symptoms. The list of symptoms prepared for *DSM IV* shows more school-related behavior than the list from *DSM III-R.*

Final DSM-IV Draft Criteria for Attention Deficit Hyperactivity Disorder

A. Either 1 or 2:

    (1) Inattention: At least six of the following symptoms of inattention have persisted for at least six months to a degree that is maladaptive and inconsistent with developmental level:

        (a) Often fails to give close attention to details or makes careless mistakes in school-work, work, or other activities

        (b) Often has difficulty sustaining attention in tasks or play activities

        (c) Often does not seem to listen to what is being said to him or her

        (d) Often does not follow through on instructions and fails to finish schoolwork, chores, or duties in the workplace (not due to oppositional behavior or failure to understand instructions)

        (e) Often has difficulties organizing tasks and activities

        (f) Often avoids or strongly dislikes tasks (such as schoolwork or homework) that require sustained mental effort

        (g) Often loses things necessary for tasks or activities (e.g., school assignments, pencils, books, tools, or toys)

        (h) Is often easily distracted by extraneous stimuli

        (i) Often forgetful in daily activities

    (2) Hyperactivity-Impulsivity: At least six of the following symptoms of hyperactivity-impulsivity have persisted for at least six months to a degree that is maladaptive and inconsistent with developmental level:

    Hyperactivity

        (a) Often fidgets with hands or feet or squirms in seat

        (b) Leaves seat in classroom or in other situations in which remaining seated is expected

        (c) Often runs about or climbs excessively in situations where it is inappropriate (in adolescents or adults, may be limited to subjective feelings of restlessness)

        (d) Often has difficulty playing or engaging in leisure activities quietly

        (e) Often talks excessively

        (f) Often acts as if "driven by a motor" and cannot remain still

    Impulsivity

        (g) Often blurts out answers to questions before the questions have been completed

        (h) Often has difficulty waiting in lines or awaiting turn in games or group situations

        (i) Often interrupts or intrudes on others

B. Onset no later than seven years of age.

C. Symptoms must be present in two or more situations (e.g., at school, work, and at home).

D. The disturbance causes clinically significant distress or impairment in social, academic, or occupational functioning.

E. Does not occur exclusively during the course of a Pervasive Developmental Disorder, Schizophrenia, or other Psychotic Disorder, and is not better accounted for by a Mood Disorder, Anxiety Disorder, Dissociative Disorder, or a Personality Disorder.

Code based on type:

    314.00 Attention-deficit/Hyperactivity Disorder, Predominantly Inattentive Type; if criterion A(1) is met but not criterion A(2) for the past six months

    314.01 Attention-deficit/Hyperactivity Disorder, Predominantly Hyperactive-Impulsive Type: if criterion A(2) is met but not criterion A(1) for the past six months

    314.01 Attention-deficit/Hyperactivity Disorder, Combined Type; if both criterion A(1) and A(2) are met for the past six months

Coding note: for individuals (especially adolescents and adults) who currently have symptoms that no longer meet full criteria, "in partial remission" should be specified.

    314.9 Attention-deficit/Hyperactivity Disorder Not Otherwise Specified

    This category is for disorders with prominent symptoms of attention-deficit or hyperactivity-impulsivity that do not meet criteria for Attention Deficit/Hyperactivity Disorder.

Keith McBurnett, Benjamin Lahey, and Linda J. Piffner, "Diagnosis of Attention Deficit Disorders in DSM-IV: Scientific Basis and Implications for Education," *Exceptional Children,* Vol. 60, No. 2 (October/November, 1993), 113. Reprinted by permission of the publisher.

Characteristics of Attention Deficit Hyperactivity Disorder

A major work on attention deficit hyperactivity disorder (ADHD) provides a source for discussion of the significance of this disorder for education. See the "Special Issue: Issues in the Education of Children with Attention Deficit Disorder," *Exceptional Children,* Vol. 60, No. 2 (October/November, 1993). The entire issue and particularly the article by Sydney Zentall provide a valuable resource.[1]

Areas of learning that cause difficulties for children with ADHD are listed next. These children may have:

1. Difficulty while listening in selecting and attending to a message while ignoring background auditory stimulation or competing information
2. Difficulty in attending to a basic message when much detail or less essential explanations are added (These children prefer global cues ["it looks like"] over additional detail ["it has these parts"].)
3. Difficulty in responding when asked unless external cues, such as pictures or visual cues, are presented (However, these students become talkative when they initiate a conversation.)
4. Difficulty in comprehending long passages to be read but less likely to have vocabulary deficits
5. Other disabilities, such as dyslexia, which may account for the reading difficulties of these students
6. Difficulty in computing because of problems in handling multiple operations, organizing verbal information, eliminating extraneous information, and being attentive to repetition
7. Difficulties in maintaining clear handwriting the longer the time spent on a task in an activity, especially copying

As with dyslexia, attention deficits often occur in tandem with other learning disabilities. Based on much observation and on reports from students, careful planning is required for combining interventions with classroom accommodations that the teacher and class can support. Students' success in the general classroom will depend on a variety of settings and presentations that help students to select appropriate stimuli, manage extraneous stimuli, and control impulsive behaviors.

Medication for Attention Deficit Hyperactivity Disorder

One additional approach more often used with students with ADHD is monitoring of medication. An enormous amount of scientific literature is available on the use of stimulant medication to treat children with attention deficit disorder. The scope of this chapter does not include such a discussion. The teacher has a major role in cooperating with the parent or caregiver in monitoring the behavior of a student receiving medication for ADHD and in systematically reporting changes in behavior so that the teacher, parent, and physician are equally aware of the results from such observations.

---

[1]This material was adapted from Sydney S. Zentall, "Research on the Educational Implications of Attention Deficit Hyperactivity Disorder," *Exceptional Children,* Vol. 60, No. 2 (October/November, 1993), 143–53.

Research Centers for Attention Deficit Disorder

The Division of Innovation and Development, Office of Special Education Programs, Office of Special Education and Rehabilitative Services, U.S. Department of Education (USDOE), has funded five centers to review research and educational practices with children with ADD. Some early summaries of these reviews do not provide much information on educational interventions. Because the research on behavioral and educational interventions for children with ADD was more frequently done in clinical rather than in school settings, it is unclear how well the techniques will transfer to the classroom. The initial work has centered on seven topics relevant to educators: positive reinforcement (tokens); behavior reduction (redirection); response cost (removing tokens); self-instruction or cognitive-behavioral training (behavior modification with cognitive strategies); parent or family training (continuance at home); tasks or environmental stimulation (increased stimulus values); and biofeedback.

As the work of the centers progresses, schools may receive increased guidance from the results of the studies. Parents and teachers who want more information might watch for future publications from the Office of Special Education and Rehabilitative Services, USDOE, or from such journals as *Exceptional Children*, which published a special edition on ADD, cited on the preceding page, that included articles by some authors whose work was funded by the USDOE projects.

Strategies for assisting students with ADD and ADHD can be found in Chapter II under "Students' Attention Span," "Organizational Skills," and "Appropriate Social Skills." Some other possibilities are suggested in the next section, "Students' Behavior."

Additional Information on Attention Deficit Disorder

Appendix C, "Characteristics of Children with Attention Disorders," by Edna D. Copeland, contains material to help educators recognize symptoms of attention disorders. Three categories of major problems are examined: inattention, impulsivity, and problems with activity level—either overactivity or underactivity. Other problems discussed are noncompliance, attention-getting behavior, immaturity, school problems, emotional difficulties, poor peer relations, and family interaction problems.

Students' Behavior

This section examines a positive approach to dealing with students' behavior. The hypothesis supporting this approach is that children use unacceptable behavior to support acceptable ideas, feelings, and emotions. The process for developing positive behavioral support is designed to (1) define the students' behavior; (2) develop hypotheses for the communicative intent of the behavior; (3) identify the corresponding skill deficit; and (4) develop appropriate teaching strategies.

Support for Students

During the past ten years, many research studies have been done to understand students' behavior better so that schools can respond positively. This nationwide movement comes from groups that want to restrict the use of punishment. As dependency on punish-

Note: Larry W. Douglass provided the material on "Students' Behavior."

ment declines, replacement behaviors and strategies must be offered to parents and teachers of students with learning disabilities and behavioral challenges. This new direction has brought about innovative interpretations for all behaviors regardless of a student's disability. Although this process can potentially benefit all students, it appears to be especially appropriate for learning disabilities.

The Working Hypothesis

New research has shown that many students, regardless of their disabilities, use nonverbal *acting out* or *withdrawn* behaviors to express reasonable feelings and emotions. Many students have learned unacceptable ways to express acceptable ideas, feelings, and emotions. These students cannot be faulted for having these ideas or emotions or for having learned unacceptable forms of expression. Parents and teachers are the ones most likely to encounter those unacceptable forms that children have devised to tell about their experiences, problems, and dilemmas. Parents and teachers react by labeling these expressions "inappropriate" and "unacceptable." From what is understood about students with learning handicaps, educators can recognize these students' difficulties in language acquisition and learning. The struggle that educators and parents face, however, is to help these students learn acceptable ways of expressing their ideas, emotions, or feelings.

The Process

The steps in this new positive behavioral support process appear in the flowchart that follows:

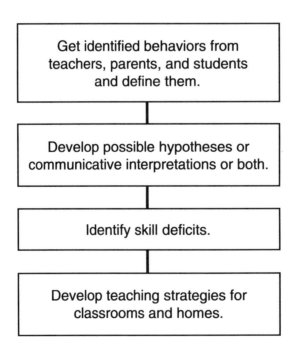

Get identified behaviors from teachers, parents, and students and define them.

Develop possible hypotheses or communicative interpretations or both.

Identify skill deficits.

Develop teaching strategies for classrooms and homes.

Step one: defining students' behavior. This new way of understanding students' behavior is based on a process with four specific steps. To begin this process correctly, one must honestly clarify the problem behavior. At this early stage it is not important to critique its seriousness or inappropriateness. In most cases teachers and parents have tried many different approaches before informing others of the problem. But it is vitally important to pinpoint the behavior so that others working with the student can describe and recognize it. Being overly vague and general is not fair at this point. It is important to be specific. Exact descriptions will help teachers and parents as well as students.

Step two: developing hypotheses around the communicative intent of the behavior. At this point we will venture outside of procedures for normal behavioral analysis to try to find the possible communicative hypotheses for the identified behaviors. Pooling our resources and knowledge, we next consider the problem behavior. It is best to use *I statements,* believing that the students are actually using their behaviors to communicate. In this section a common behavioral problem, "talks out in class," is examined. We will use the behavior and its accompanying hypotheses listed in the example that follows to demonstrate the other steps in the process of positive behavioral support.

Behavior Problem	*Possible Communicative Functions and Hypotheses*
Talks out in class	*I have an idea, and I must tell someone, so I . . .*
	I don't get called on, so I . . .
	My ideas are very important to me, so I . . .
	I don't have a storage system; I don't want to lose my ideas, so I . . .
	I want to disrupt the class, so I . . .
	I am a good talker, and I want to be known for my strengths, so I . . .
	I know this really bothers my teacher, so I . . .
	I want others to lose, so I . . .
	I think and process by talking, so I . . .

The purpose of this step is to expand our thinking and vision about the problem behavior. In most cases teachers and parents have exhausted their strategies before they seek behavioral consultation. To counter this delay effectively, we need to increase the number of possibilities for understanding the behavior. At the end of this step, we have added possibly dozens of potential interpretations to the list. However, this step must not be taken by an individual—a parent or a teacher. The development of a full and wholesome list of interpretations depends on brainstorming by a group.

Before moving on, we must understand what makes this list critical to maintaining a positive approach. The good things about this list are that it:

- Is balanced (Some aspects are good, and some are not.)
- Acknowledges behavior as communication
- Formalizes what most teachers do each minute or day
- Expands thinking about students' behavior
- Links language problems and behavior in students with learning disabilities
- Moves away from behavioral modification and becomes aligned more with teaching

Before any decisions are made about any list of hypotheses, it must be given to people who know the student well—teachers, parents, and the student. The chosen hypotheses become the focus of the intervention.

Step three: identification of the corresponding skill deficit. The next step is to identify the student's skill deficit that corresponds to the chosen hypothesis. Examples of several hypotheses and the reasons for those choices are as follows:

Scenario A. A child's parents who select the hypothesis: "I am a good talker, and I want to be known for my strengths" are admitting that their child has a talent for speech. In addition, the parents are acknowledging their child's difficulty in recognizing additional personal strengths and skills. The child's deficit would be a lack of ability to see himself or herself as skilled in any other areas. The child is capable of recognizing a single strength—talking—but has a narrow vision of his or her other capacities.

Scenario B. On the other hand, if the teacher identifies "the student's lack of a storage system" as the hypothesis, the deficit would be defined as a lack of an organized pattern for mentally saving and retrieving one's thoughts and ideas. The child clearly has the skills for forming thoughts and ideas. But problems arise after those thoughts and ideas have been formulated because the child cannot hold those thoughts until later.

Scenario C. If the student identifies the communicative intent as "I don't get called on, so I talk out in class," the problem would be completely different. The deficit might be identified as the child's not recognizing times when he or she is called on or not recognizing how he or she could gain the teacher's attention and acceptance through means other than talking out in class.

As the preceding three scenarios show, hypotheses for different communicative intents may identify unique corresponding deficits. Nonetheless, we have supported our process by carefully selecting the appropriate hypothesis before we move forward in our design of an intervention.

Step four: development of teaching strategies for interventions from the school and home. It is now appropriate to develop teaching strategies or curriculum modifications to affect the chosen hypothesis and the corresponding skill deficit. To understand this step fully, we return to the sample scenarios:

Scenario A. The parents' choice of "I am a good talker, and I want to be known for my strengths" would lead to the development of an intervention specific to this selection. It would seem natural to assist this student in identifying and developing additional strengths and capacities. Being able to "shine" in other ways would allow the student to be more relaxed in his or her need to talk out in class.

Scenario B. The teacher identifies the lack of "an effective storage system." The goal of the teachers will be to teach the student how to store and retrieve important thoughts and ideas. This activity might be accomplished with a pad and paper. Or the student might need a tape recorder to transcribe his or her thoughts and ideas. Whatever the intervention, it must specifically match the hypothesis of choice.

Scenario C. The student identifies the hypothesis "I don't get called on, so I talk out in class." Instead of waiting and hoping for recognition from the teacher, the student merely talks out whenever the need arises. A recording system might be designed whereby the student is responsible for collecting data on *times called on* and *times others are called on.* Likewise, the student might be shown how he or she could get the teacher's recognition by completing assignments and helping others. The goal of the teachers would be to equate these episodes with being called on in class. Once again, the student should learn to be more relaxed about the need to talk out in class.

Summary

Using the specific example presented in this section and keeping true to the notion that the problem behavior is nonverbal communication, we have followed this process from its logical beginning to an understandable outcome. Principles of positive behavioral support were applied showing how three interventions were developed that are atypical of most behavior modification programs. If correct procedures have been followed, the student will have learned new skills to match the identified deficit; and an intervention will have been developed that is contrary to more traditional methods of behavioral management. For the student with learning disabilities, a process has been followed that more closely adheres to what is known about those students—that their problems in learning language can be identified. Lastly, we have honestly acknowledged language from the student typically labeled "language challenged." We are on a new path that will improve our understanding of students with learning disabilities while at the same time encouraging these same students to develop and refine their rudimentary forms of communication. In pursuing this path, neither we nor the students can lose.

Context of the Process

The process outlined in this section was developed in the light of concerns that were codified in Assembly Bill 2586 (Hughes, 1990) as *Education Code* sections 56520–56524 and in *California Code of Regulations* sections 3001 and 3052 relating to positive behavioral interventions. However, the process has broader applicability for all teachers, especially for teachers of individuals with exceptional needs who may have behavioral goals and objectives but do not require a behavioral intervention plan.

For further information on this process, contact the Special Education Division, California Department of Education.

Questions and Answers

Is it true that all dyslexics see things backwards and upside down?

No. Although one pattern commonly seen in the spelling and sometimes the reading of dyslexic students is the presence of reversals, transpositions, and inversions of letters or numbers, research continues to indicate that dyslexics do not see things backwards. The occurrence of reversed or transposed letters or both seems more related to neurological processing than to sight.

If a child is able to read, does that mean that he or she is not dyslexic?

No. Some dyslexic children can read but have significant difficulty with spelling, handwriting, reading comprehension or development of written composition skills or with all four skills.

If I make my dyslexic child read to me for 20 minutes each night, will that help him or her to learn how to read?

It depends. Dyslexic children with reading deficits need direct, professional instruction in the mechanics of written language before practice in reading will help to build reading skills. Often, when a dyslexic child, who does not yet understand the code of written language is forced to read, the child will likely develop a dislike of reading.

If a dyslexic child is beginning to read, the child should be reading books that are at a phonetic level equivalent to the child's reading abilities. It is of the utmost importance that the child experience an emotionally safe environment in which to practice reading skills. If the child's reading errors or difficulties create parental tension, the child should read aloud with a helping professional while skills are being built.

The parents of a dyslexic child should be encouraged to read to the child regularly. Reading to dyslexic children is helpful toward building vocabulary and other important basic reading skills.

Will colored or tinted lenses cure my child's dyslexia?

No. Results from scientific research studies have not indicated that the use of colored lenses cures dyslexia. Past and current research studies on the brain indicate that dyslexia is a complex syndrome that affects multiple areas of language processing. The most long-term and fully researched remedies for dyslexia involve direct instruction in development of written language skills.

However, increasing evidence reveals that some children with dyslexia experience visual distortions, especially while reading, that seem to be associated with a sensitivity to light and perhaps to color and contrast. For these children the use of colored lenses does appear to reduce specific visual distortions and visual fatigue. Parents and teachers should be aware, however, that research is still ongoing regarding this phenomenon and that colored lenses should not be viewed as a primary intervention for a dyslexic child.

Sources Cited

Aaron, P. G. 1989. *Dyslexia and Hyperlexia.* Dordrecht, The Netherlands: Kluwer Academic Publishers.

Aaron, P. G., and Catherine Baker. 1991. *Reading Disabilities in College and High School: Diagnosis and Management.* Parkland, Md.: York Press.

Chall, Jeanne S. 1987. *Intimacy with Language: A Forgotten Basic in Teacher Evaluation.* Baltimore, Md.: The Orton Dyslexia Society.

Critchley, Macdonald. 1968. London: World Federation of Neurology. (April 3–5). Memorandum.

Galaburda, M.D., Albert M. 1989. "Ordinary and Extraordinary Brain Development: Anatomical Variation in Developmental Dyslexia." *Annals of Dyslexia,* Vol. 39, 67–80.

Goldstein, Sam, and Michael Goldstein. 1992. *A Teacher's Guide: Attention Deficit Hyperactivity Disorder in Children* (Second edition). Salt Lake City: The Neurology, Learning, and Behavior Center.

Green, Jane Fell. 1993. "Psycholinguistic Assessment: Critical Components in Identifying Dyslexia." Paper presented at the 44th International Conference of the Orton Dyslexia Society, November 4, at New Orleans.

Livingstone, Margaret S., and others. 1991. "Physiological and Anatomical Evidence for a Magnocellular Defect in Developmental Dyslexia." *Proceedings of the National Academy of Sciences of the United States of America.* Vol. 88, No. 18 (September 15), 7943–47.

McBurnett, Keith; Benjamin Lahey; and Linda J. Piffner. 1993. "Diagnosis of Attention Deficit Disorders in DSM-IV: Scientific Basis and Implications for Education." *Exceptional Children.* Vol. 60, No. 2 (October/November), 108–17.

Silver, M.D., Larry B. N.d. *ADHD Attention Deficit-Hyperactivity Disorder and Learning Disabilities.* Booklet for the Classroom Teacher. Summit, N.J.: CIBA-GEIGY.

Slingerland, Beth. 1982. *Specific Language–Not Learning–Disability Children.* Cambridge, Mass.: Educators Publishing Service, Inc.

Zentall, Sydney S. 1993. "Research on the Educational Implications of Attention Deficit Hyperactivity Disorder." *Exceptional Children.* Vol. 60, No. 2 (October/November), 143–53.

Selected References on Dyslexia

Aaron, P. G. *Dyslexia and Hyperplexia.* Dordecht, the Netherlands: Kluwer Academic Publishers, 1989.

Aaron, P. G., and Catherine Baker. *Reading Disabilities in College and High School: Diagnosis and Management.* Parkland, Md.: York Press, 1991.

Blachman, Benita A. "An Alternative Classroom Reading Program for Learning Disabled and Other Low-Achieving Children," in *Intimacy with Language: A Forgotten Basic in Teacher Education.* Edited by Rosemary Bowler. Baltimore: The Orton Dyslexia Society, 1987, pp. 49–55.

Chall, Jeanne S. "The Importance of Instruction in Reading Methods for All Teachers," in *Intimacy with Language: A Forgotten Basic in Teacher Education.* Edited by Rosemary Bowler. Baltimore: The Orton Dyslexia Society, 1987, pp. 15–23.

Clark, Diana B. *Dyslexia: Theory and Practice of Remedial Instruction.* Parkton, Md.: York Press, Inc., 1988.

De Hirsch, Katrina; Jeannette Jansky; and William Langford. *Predicting Reading Failure.* New York: Harper & Row Publishers, Inc., 1966.

Duane, Drake D. "Commentary on Dyslexia and Neurodevelopmental Pathology," *Journal of Learning Disabilities,* Vol. 22, No. 4 (April, 1989), 219–20.

Dyslexia and Development: Neurobiological Aspects of Extraordinary Brains. Edited by Albert M. Galaburda, M.D. Cambridge, Mass.: Harvard University Press, 1993.

Galaburda, M.D., Albert M., "Ordinary and Extraordinary Brain Development: Anatomical Variation in Developmental Dyslexia," *Annals of Dyslexia,* Vol. 39 (1989), 67–80.

Geschwind, Norman. "Why Orton Was Right," *Annals of Dyslexia,* Vol. 32 (1982), 13–30.

Gillingham, Anna, and Bessie W. Stillman. *Remedial Training for Children with Specific Disability in Reading, Spelling, and Penmanship.* Cambridge, Mass.: Educators Publishing Service, Inc., 1988.

Goldstein, Sam, and Michael Goldstein, M.D. *A Teacher's Guide: Attention Deficit Hyperactivity Disorder in Children* (Second edition). Salt Lake City: The Neurology, Learning, and Behavior Center, 1992.

Green, Jane Fell. "Psycholinguistic Assessment: Critical Components in Identifying Dyslexia." Paper presented to the 44th International Conference of the Orton Dyslexia Society, New Orleans, November 4, 1993.

Hugdahl, K. "Functional Brain Asymmetry, Dyslexia, and Immune Disorders," in *Dyslexia and Development: Neurobiological Aspects of Extraordinary Brains.* Edited by Albert M. Galaburda, M.D. Cambridge, Mass.: Harvard University Press, 1993, pp. 113–33.

Liberman, Isabel Y. "Language and Literacy: The Obligation of the Schools of Education," in *Intimacy with Language: A Forgotten Basic in Teacher Education.* Edited by Rosemary Bowler. Baltimore: The Orton Dyslexia Society, 1987, pp. 1–9.

Livingstone, Margaret S., and others. "Physiological and Anatomical Evidence for a Magnocellular Defect in Developmental Dyslexia," *Proceedings of the National Academy of Sciences of the United States of America,* Vol. 88, No. 18 (September 15, 1991), 7943–47.

Pennington, Bruce F. *Diagnosing Learning Disorders: A Neuropsychological Framework.* New York: Guilford Press, 1991.

Rawson, Margaret B. *The Many Faces of Dyslexia.* Cambridge, Mass.: Educators Publishing Service, Inc., 1986.

Reading Disorders in the United States. Report of the Secretary's National Advisory Committee on Dyslexia and Related Reading Disorders. Bethesda, Md.: U.S. Department of Health, Education, and Welfare, 1969. ERIC, ED 037317.

Silver, M.D., Larry B., *ADHD Attention Deficit Hyperactivity Disorder and Learning Disabilities.* Booklet for the Classroom Teacher. Summit, N.J.: CIBA-GEIGY, n.d.

Slingerland, Beth. *A Multisensory Approach to Language Arts for Specific Language Disability Children.* Cambridge, Mass.: Educators Publishing Service, Inc., 1992.

Slingerland, Beth. *Specific Language—Not Learning—Disability Children.* Cambridge, Mass.: Educators Publishing Service, Inc., 1982.

Slingerland, Beth. *Why Wait for a Criterion of Failure?* Cambridge, Mass.: Educators Publishing Service, Inc., 1974.

Vail, Priscilla L. *About Dyslexia: Unraveling the Myth.* Rosemont, N.J.: Modern Learning Press, 1990.

Vail, Priscilla L. "Gifts, Talents, and the Dyslexias: Wellsprings, Springboards, and Finding Foley's Rocks," *Annals of Dyslexia,* Vol. 40 (1990), 3–17.

West, Thomas G. *In the Mind's Eye: Visual Thinkers, Gifted People with Learning Difficulties, Computer Images, and the Ironies of Creativity.* Buffalo, N.Y.: Prometheus Books, 1991.

Williams, Joanna. "Educational Treatments for Dyslexia at the Elementary and Secondary Levels," in *Intimacy with Language: A Forgotten Basic in Teacher Education.* Edited by Rosemary Bowler. Baltimore: The Orton Dyslexia Society, 1987, pp. 24–32.

PART TWO

Gathering the Team— Finding Solutions

CHAPTER IV

Referral, Assessment, and Eligibility for Special Education Services

This chapter contains practical information about referring students to special education services, assessing students, and determining their eligibility for special education services. The referral process is discussed. The steps in the assessment process are addressed as well as the uses of assessment information. Also discussed is the use of assessment information to help the student who has experienced difficulties in learning or performance and who the IEP team has determined is not eligible for special education services. Using assessment information to help students having difficulties becomes more and more important as the student population in our schools becomes increasingly diverse. Provisions from the Education Code regarding eligibility are cited.

Content and Organization

The section on the referral process contains information on the content of a referral, referral by school staff, referral by a parent, and steps that follow a referral. Topics discussed as a part of the assessment process are essential elements of the assessment process, assessment of language minority and dialect-speaking students, legal time lines, the assessment plan, assessment procedures, assessment materials and tests, assessment personnel, assessment report, parental notification of findings, and parental rights to an independent assessment. Specific procedures and criteria as well as strategies for the use of the criteria are given in the section on "Eligibility for Special Education Services." Finally, questions and answers are included to inform the reader about common problems in assessing and referring students and in determining their eligibility.

The Referral Process

Referral is a necessary step if students are to be considered eligible for special education services. Students having problems with learning in the regular education program should have their activities considered for modification before referral. If the resources of the regular education program have been applied and found to be inappropriate or ineffective, then the students may be referred for special education to determine the nature and extent of their disability and a plan for their education.

Content of a Referral

Education Code Section 56029 states that "'Referral for assessment' means any written request for assessment to identify an individual with exceptional needs made by a parent, teacher, or other service provider." A referral formally requests that a student be thoroughly assessed in all areas related to the suspected learning problem. The assessment may or may not result in a student's becoming eligible for special education and related services.

Referral by School Staff

A referral may be made by the school staff. The parent must be provided with a written notice of the intent to refer. This notice is not required if the parent is a member of the student study team recommending referral or personally requests the referral. The referral must include a brief reason for the referral and documentation of the resources of the regular education program that have been considered and modified. The referral must also include the results of the intervention. The school's approach is questionable when the first attempt at intervention is the teacher's advising the parents to refer their child for special education.

The reason for the referral and the description of attempted modifications may be combined in one statement. Often, the reason for referral is that the attempted modifications have not succeeded. The child may be experiencing increasing frustration that further interferes with classroom processes.

Referral by a Parent

A parent who wishes to make a referral should provide a written request asking for an assessment specifically for consideration of special education services. The request should be sent to the teacher, principal, or special education administrative office. When a parent makes an oral request for a referral, staff of the school district, special education local plan area, or county office must help the parent make a written request. If the parent requests assistance, the school's staff must provide it.

After Referral

A written referral for assessment, which is the first step in the special education process, begins the time line for the other steps. According to *Education Code* Section 56321(a), within 15 calendar days of the referral, the parent must be given a written proposed assessment plan. It must include an explanation of the right to a due process hearing and other procedural safeguards.

The Assessment Process

Once the procedures for the formal referral have been completed, the assessment process begins. *Education Code* Section 56320 states that "before any action is taken with respect to the initial placement of an individual with exceptional needs in special education instruction, an individual assessment of the pupil's educational needs shall be conducted . . . ." This assessment process includes several essential elements:

- Specific time lines
- Procedures
- Requirements regarding testing personnel, parental notification, testing instruments, and so forth

Essential Elements of the Assessment Process

In general, assessment is conducted by various professionals at the school site who collect data that will be used to:

- Identify strengths and weaknesses pertinent to a learner's educational success.
- Help the IEP team decide eligibility for special education and related services.
- Assist the general and special education teacher in determining appropriate strategies for instructing students who *do not* meet eligibility criteria.
- Develop an individualized education program (IEP) for students who *do* meet eligibility criteria.

The primary goal of assessment is to gather information to better meet the educational needs of a student who is not successful in school. By conducting an in-depth inspection of a pupil's learning styles, cognitive abilities, and academic and social skills, the assessment team becomes responsible for collecting and sharing information. This information is used by general educators and special educators to facilitate successful, productive learning experiences. In other words, *the main purpose of assessment is not to label a youngster as having or not having a disability but, instead, to help teachers educate students who are experiencing difficulty in the classroom.*

With this concept in mind, one must understand that assessment and evaluation are continuing activities that should be taking place long before a pupil is referred for a formal assessment. All of the interventions already presented in a student's learning program should be monitored and evaluated regularly. When the formal assessment process takes place, the assessment team assumes that the interventions tried previously were inadequate. If the results from the completed assessment process determine that a student does not qualify for special education and related services, information about the results must be communicated clearly to the referring general education teacher, allowing him or her to modify instructional interventions accordingly.

Assessment of Language-Minority and Dialect-Speaking Students

California's limited-English-speaking (LEP) population continues to increase, creating a need for more assessment services for these students. The assessment team often has to determine whether an LEP student is experiencing a language disorder or whether slow second-language acquisition or limited school experiences cause the linguistic deficits. A student classified as fluent-English proficient (FEP) has achieved a basic level of English fluency and should be able to benefit from English instruction. Assessment may be conducted in English. However, the classification *FEP does not mean that the student is English dominant; that is,* FEP *does not mean that the student functions better in English than in his or her primary language.* Nonstandardized assessment in the primary language may still be necessary.

Students classified as limited-English proficient (LEP) do not possess sufficient English language skills to benefit, without support, from instruction only in English; for example, they need English language development or bilingual education.

To determine whether a language disorder exists, the assessment team must use data derived from the student's linguistic functioning level in his or her primary language. A student may not be identified as language disordered solely because he or she is not familiar with English. An LEP student must be assessed in his or her primary language. However, baseline data regarding English language performance are also necessary. This information will help team members develop appropriate educational plans.

A student is classified as English only (EO) when certain members of his or her family speak a language other than English, but the student speaks only English. Those students are most appropriately assessed in English because their fluency in another language is minimal. Cultural factors must be given equal consideration in the assessment process.

Legal Time Lines

Before a referral for assessment has been initiated, parents must be notified. An assessment plan must be created within 15 calendar days of the actual referral. When the parents have received this information, they have at least an additional 15 days to decide whether to consent to the proposed assessment. If the parents provide consent, personnel from the local educational agency (LEA) or special educational local plan area (SELPA) have 50 calendar days in which to conduct an assessment and develop an IEP. *A formal assessment may not be initiated without parental consent.*

The Assessment Plan

According to *Education Code* Section 56321, a proposed assessment plan will be created and sent to the parents for approval, along with a copy of the notice of parents' rights. A good practice is to have the assessor personally explain the assessment plan to the parent.

The assessment plan should include the following:

- Be [written] in language easily understood by the general public.
- Be provided in the primary language [or other mode of communication] of the parent.
- Explain the types of assessments to be conducted.
- State [explicitly] that no individualized education program will result from the assessment without the consent of the parent.

Additionally, regulations require that the assessment plan include "any available independent assessments and any assessment information the parent requests to be considered . . ." (*California Code of Regulations, Title 5, Education,* Section 3022). And, finally, the assessment plan should specifically indicate the pupil's primary language as well as his or her proficiency.

Assessment Procedures

As discussed previously, the main goal of the assessment process is to provide information to the general educator or special educator or both that will allow them to design and implement successful educational interventions for students experiencing academic difficulty or failure. Professional educators advocate the following three general approaches to assessment:

1. Assessing the learner
2. Determining the compatibility between the learner and the instruction (both the current instruction and the instruction being recommended)
3. Determining the compatibility between the learner and the instructional environment

Although the first approach is the most popular one, it is not usually sufficient—especially for meeting a student's educational needs.

Before a referral is made to the assessment team, factors in the environment should be examined and evaluated; for example, compatibility between the learner and the instructional method and compatibility between the learner and the instructional environment. Often, during this prereferral stage the teacher may ask other school personnel, such as the school psychologist, special education teacher, or speech and language specialist, to visit the classroom, observe the student, and offer suggestions for modifying the instruction or environment. Whenever possible throughout the prereferral stages, both the student and the parent should be consulted regarding their ideas for helpful strategies and interventions.

If the student still does not succeed academically after the suggested modifications or interventions have been tried, a referral is made. The assessment team examines factors unique to the learner to gain information about the student's modality of learning (for example, visual, auditory, or kinesthetic), academic and social strengths, and weaknesses. The first goal of the in-depth assessment is to provide the referring teacher with additional information that might assist in the design and delivery of improved educational interventions. If the student qualifies for special education services as well, then those services are determined by the IEP team. But the mission of the assessment process is not to label pupils but to provide information. Formal assessment is conducted to help teachers educate students who are experiencing difficulty or failure in school.

Regarding formal assessment, one should note that *Education Code* Section 56320(e) clearly states that "no single procedure [should be] used as the sole criterion for determining an appropriate educational program for an individual" suspected of having specific learning disabilities, dyslexia, attention deficits, or other related disorders. Furthermore, the following areas related to suspected specific learning disabilities, dyslexia, attention deficits, or other related disorders must be assessed when appropriate: "health and development, vision, including low vision, hearing, motor abilities, language function, general ability, academic performance, self-help, orientation and mobility skills, career and vocational abilities and interests, and social and emotional status" (see *Education Code* Section 56320[f]). In other words, a comprehensive assessment must be conducted, examining more than simple academic performance.

The scope of the assessment should be comprehensive while ensuring that all testing and assessment materials are free from racial, cultural, or gender bias. Furthermore, *the assessment team may not diagnose "the normal process of second-language acquisition" as a specific learning disability, dyslexia, attention deficits, or other related disorders.*

And, finally, all students should have hearing and vision screening unless parental permission has not been obtained for such tests.

Assessment Materials and Tests

No single test identifies learning disabilities, dyslexia, or attention deficit. Therefore, members of the assessment team employ a variety of formal and informal assessment techniques. Formal assessment typically refers to standardized tests that are primarily used to compare the performance of the individual with the performance of his or her peer group (the norm sample). (Standardized tests are also referred to as "norm-referenced" tests.) Tests are usually selected on the basis of their technical adequacy, which encompasses their validity (the degree to which the test actually measures what it says it measures); their reliability (the degree to which the test will give a similar score if the test were retaken); and the adequacy of their norms (the comparison group). Also, tests are examined for the possibility of ethnic, cultural, and gender bias.

Another type of formal assessment the team uses is criterion-referenced testing, which measures a pupil's development of particular skills in terms of absolute levels of mastery. In other words, the tests determine the degree to which a student can perform certain academic tasks.

Parents and professionals should be aware of other terms or labels that have been used to refer to assessment practices that are in some way connected to criterion-referenced tests; for example, *curriculum-based assessment, objective-referenced assessment, direct and frequent measurement, direct assessment,* and *formative evaluation of students' progress.* Students' work samples are collected in combination with information gathered from criterion-referenced tests. *Portfolio assessment* is based on analyzing actual samples of a pupil's academic work. *Authentic assessment* involves analyzing a student's progress using tasks that would be typical of what he or she would be required to do in class or in the real world. *Ecological assessment* involves the total environment that affects the student.

Using both norm-referenced and criterion-referenced measures, assessment personnel identify the pupil's current level of performance, gain insight regarding learning styles and strategies, and locate potential causes for lack of academic success.

Informal assessment is more qualitative compared to formal procedures. Generally, informal assessment refers to nonstandard methods used to pinpoint a student's educational strengths and weaknesses. The teacher uses nonstandard measures in the classroom almost daily. The following types of materials are included:

- Tests and quizzes
- Behavior checklists and inventories
- Rating scales
- Seat-work exercises
- Orally administered exercises
- Informal teaching lessons
- Individually administered written assignments

Results obtained from informal assessment procedures provide the qualitative detail lacking in formal procedures, filling in the missing parts of a student's learning profile.

Once this profile is complete, the teacher can use instructional interventions ultimately to meet a student's educational needs. These interventions are not necessarily new ones. They may have been tried previously and then modified on the basis of new information gained from the formal assessment process.

All tests and assessment materials must meet specific requirements if they are to be used to measure a pupil's aptitude and achievement. First, tests must be administered in the student's primary language or mode of communication. Second, all tests must "have been validated for the specific purpose for which they are used" (see *Education Code* Section 56320[b][2]). Finally, all tests must be administered by trained personnel.

As far as actual test scores are concerned, norm-referenced (standardized) test scores are usually reported in one of five ways: (1) grade-equivalent scores; (2) age-equivalent scores; (3) intelligence quotients; (4) standard scores; or (5) percentile ranks. Criterion-referenced scores, on the other hand, are usually reported as a percent-correct score, thereby indicating a student's relative mastery of a specific skill. Consequently, formal assessment measures, such as the two types of tests previously mentioned, yield quantitative scores, whereas informal assessment measures report information in a more qualitative manner.

Assessment Personnel

One question often asked by parents and teachers at the beginning of the assessment process is, "Who is allowed to administer tests to my child/student?" *Education Code* Section 56322 states that "the assessment shall be conducted by persons [deemed] competent to perform the assessment, as determined by the school district, county office, or special education local plan area." Furthermore, the *Education Code* has also identified professionals responsible for specific areas of assessment: "Any psychological assessment of pupils . . . shall be conducted by a credentialed school psychologist . . . " (see *Education Code* Section 56324[a]). "Any health assessment of pupils . . . shall be conducted by a credentialed school nurse or physician . . . " (see *Education Code* Section 56324[b]).

Regarding limited-English-proficient (LEP) students, the *California Code of Regulations, Title 5, Education,* Section 3023, states that assessment personnel must "have a knowledge and understanding of the cultural and ethnic background of the pupil."

Assessment Report

After the appropriate personnel have completed all testing and assessment, a written document is created that reports which tests, observations, and interventions were used as well as the results obtained from these measures. The written report provides information about the following: (1) whether the student is recommended for special education and related services; (2) the basis for making such a determination; (3) all relevant observed behavior noted by the assessment team; (4) the relationship between observed behavior and the current academic and social functioning of the student; (5) all relevant family history, health, developmental, and medical findings; (6) whether or not a discrepancy between ability and achievement exists such that it cannot be corrected without special education and related services; and (7) consideration of environmental, cultural, or economic effects on learning (where appropriate). See *Education Code* Section 56327 [a–g]. The assessment report should also provide a baseline for measuring a student's progress in his or her recommended program.

Parental Notification of Findings

Once the written assessment report has been completed, *Education Code* Section 56329(a) requires that the parents of the pupil receive written notice inviting them to participate in the IEP team conference and explaining the purpose of the meeting—the discussion of assessment results and planning for educational recommendations. A date for such a meeting to take place must be scheduled. Parents may obtain, on request, a copy of the assessment findings (see *Education Code* Section 56329).

Assessment results are discussed with the parents and teacher at the IEP meeting, whereupon those present determine a student's present levels of functioning and eligibility for special education and related services. If the student is eligible, the team members determine appropriate instructional goals and objectives as well as delineate educational responsibilities among teachers and school staff. On the other hand, if a student does not qualify for special education and related services, members of the team need to communicate the findings to the referring teacher in a clear and usable fashion. Many school districts employ a group of school-site personnel, called a student study team (SST), to facilitate the communication of assessment findings and suggestions and modifications for instruction to the referring teacher.

Parental Right to an Independent Assessment

The assessment plan should encourage the parent to provide any available current assessment reports. Parents who provide independent assessment reports can have those reports considered part of the school's assessment process and by the IEP team when the members meet.

A special condition exists when the parent disagrees with the school's assessment results—either with the findings or with the extent or completeness of the assessment. In this case the parent may request an independent assessment at public expense to resolve the difference in opinion (results). The school district may challenge the request when the district believes that the assessment was appropriate by requesting a due process hearing; or the district may agree to pay for a mutually acceptable independent assessment by qualified persons.

In either case assessment results, regardless of whether they were obtained at public or private expense, must be considered by the IEP team in planning the education for the student.

Eligibility for Special Education Services

Eligibility for special education services for students suspected of having or determined to have specific learning disabilities, dyslexia, attention deficits, or other related disorders is based on specific criteria delineated in federal and state laws and regulations. When a student's eligibility for special education services is being determined, information from the referral and assessment is used to determine the educational needs of the student.

Criteria for Determining Eligibility

In *Education Code* Section 56337, various types of learning disabilities, including dyslexia, are not separately defined but are included within the context of a *specific learning disability*. Thus, all of the following must exist if a student assessed as having a specific learning disability is to qualify for special education and related services:

   (a) A severe discrepancy exists between the [student's] intellectual ability and achievements in one or more of the following academic areas:

      (1) Oral expression
      (2) Listening comprehension
      (3) Written expression
      (4) Basic reading skills
      (5) Reading comprehension
      (6) Mathematics calculation
      (7) Mathematics reasoning

   (b) The discrepancy is due to a disorder in one or more of the basic psychological processes and is not the result of environmental, cultural, or economic disadvantages.

The *California Code of Regulations, Title 5, Education,* Section 3030[j][1] stipulates that the "basic psychological processes include attention, visual processing, auditory processing, sensory-motor skills, [and] cognitive abilities, including association, conceptualization, and expression."

   (c) The discrepancy cannot be corrected through other regular or categorical services offered within the regular instructional program.

Education Code Section 56339 establishes eligibility for students with an attention deficit disorder or an attention deficit hyperactivity disorder under either subdivisions (f), (i), or (j) of Section 3030 of the *California Code of Regulations (CCR), Title 5, Education.*

Strategies for Use of the Criteria

Teachers and parents should be aware that although the eligibility criteria under *CCR* Section 3030(j) specifically state that a severe discrepancy must exist, the IEP team decides whether this discrepancy does in fact exist. Specific criteria appear in *CCR* Section 3030(j)(4)(A)(B)(C):

   1. When standardized tests are valid, a mathematical formula is used to demonstrate the severe discrepancy.
   2. When standardized tests are invalid, the severe discrepancy shall be measured by alternative means.
   3. Although standardized tests do not reveal that a pupil has a severe discrepancy, the IEP team may find that a severe discrepancy does exist as a result of a disorder in one or more of the basic psychological processes. Formal and informal sources of data are used to support the findings.

Many students with symptoms of dyslexia, attention deficit disorder, or related disorders may not meet eligibility criteria for special education services through the mathematical discrepancy formula, yet these same children may not be succeeding in school.

They may have high potential but mediocre academic performance. Assessment procedures for these students should include curriculum-based information, such as portfolio assessment (work samples collected systematically from students); authentic assessment (tasks are relevant to a student's real-world experience and assignments within the day-to-day school environment); and documented observation by professionals in the classroom.

Parents and teachers of students suspected of having attention deficit disorder should also be aware that these students may qualify for special education services specified in the *CCR* under the categories of "Other Health Impaired" (Section 3030[f]) or "Seriously Emotionally Disturbed" (Section 3030[i][1]–[5]).

Finally, parents and teachers should note that students with specific learning disabilities, including dyslexia, attention deficit disorder, and other related disorders, may be eligible for specialized services within the context of the regular education program through the Americans with Disabilities Act (ADA) and Section 504 of the Rehabilitation Act of 1973 (and subsequent amendments). These laws may include students who are suspected of having a disability and have been determined to be "at risk" but not in need of special education services.

Questions and Answers

What is the triennial assessment?

Even though IEPs are reviewed annually, a complete reassessment is generally not recommended because (1) a complete reassessment requires a significant amount of time, potentially detracting from the student's actual education; and (2) the validity of norm-referenced (standardized) tests is jeopardized if they are used too frequently, allowing a student possibly to memorize certain sections of particular tests.

If a student has been identified as having a specific learning disability, dyslexia, attention deficit, or other related disorders and has received special education and related services continually over a three-year period, then a complete reassessment must be conducted. In addition, a reassessment might be required if a student is not making sufficient educational progress, or if a student receiving special education may possibly be suspended or expelled.

If a child has been diagnosed through an outside assessment agency as having dyslexia and attention deficit disorder, is that child eligible for special education services?

Special education services are provided to students with dyslexia who qualify under the definition and criteria for specific learning disabilities specified in state legislation. If a student with dyslexia does not meet the criteria even after alternative assessment procedures, including independent educational assessments, have been considered, the student may still be eligible for specialized services through general education as required by the Americans with Disabilities Act, Section 504 of the Rehabilitation Act of 1973, and *Education Code* Section 56339(b). Parents should call their school district's special education administrator for details.

May a child who is experiencing academic difficulty because of attention problems yet who seems to have the ability to work within the regular classroom become eligible for and receive assistance from special education services?

The student may receive services if an IEP team determines that he or she is eligible. In this case the assessment plan should include procedures that will provide evidence that a discrepancy exists between a student's intellectual ability and academic achievement. The evidence could include results from testing; but, just as important, it should include comments from classroom observations, parents' comments, data from criterion-referenced instruments, samples of classroom work, and any other relevant information from which a significant educational discrepancy could be demonstrated.

What happens if my child is not eligible for special education services?

Students who are not eligible for special education services under current provisions may still receive modifications in the general education program, including other categorical services; or they may qualify for assistance from agencies other than school districts. For example, the student may be eligible for mental health services through a county's mental health program. The parents should also insist that the teachers, counselor, or student study team periodically review their son's or daughter's progress.

How do public schools view assessment of dyslexia?

Both federal and state laws mandate procedures for assessment of specific learning disabilities, including dyslexia. No mandated procedure exists specifically for the assessment of dyslexia. When the IEP team members are considering a student's eligibility for special education services, they must include the results from any outside assessment. The results being considered also include, but are not limited to, the assessment that determined that a student has dyslexia.

This chapter has presented descriptions of the concepts and procedures for referral and assessment of a student's educational needs. Chapter IV presents information about the individualized education program (IEP) required for each student who, as determined by an IEP team, needs special education services.

CHAPTER V

Planning and Providing Services

A student's special education services,
goals, and objectives are determined by an individualized education program (IEP) team,
members of which are the parents and professionals who work with the student. The
goals and objectives of the program are described in an individualized education program (IEP). The purpose of this chapter is to inform parents about the concept and uses
of an IEP.

Content and Organization

This chapter is divided into five sections: (1) background information on the relationship of the IEP to the provision of special education services; (2) legislative intent of the
IEP; (3) parent involvement; (4) content of an IEP; and (5) questions and answers. The
first section provides an overview of the process of developing the IEP, including information about the IEP team. The second section contains a discussion of the concept of an
IEP. The third section examines the rights of parents. The fourth section focuses on the
required contents of an IEP, including present levels of performance, goals and objectives, specific instruction and frequency of service, least restrictive environment, and
signatures of participants. The final section provides parents, school staff, and students
with answers to commonly asked questions about IEPs and the process of developing and
revising them.

Background Information

The services to be provided to students deemed eligible for special education are
determined at an individualized education program (IEP) planning meeting. The meeting
must take place within 50 calendar days of the consent for assessment, excluding days
between school sessions and terms. A student's eligibility for special education services
is based on federal and state criteria and is determined by the IEP team from the assessment of the educational needs of the student. The IEP team must include the parent or
guardian of the student; the student's present teacher; and a representative of the school
district, other than the teacher, who is knowledgeable of program options appropriate for
the student. The team may also include the pupil, if appropriate; others, at the discretion
of the parent or district, with expertise or knowledge necessary for the development of
the IEP; and individuals who have conducted an assessment of the pupil or who are
knowledgeable about assessment procedures and interpretations.

The team develops a written document known as an individualized education program (IEP). The team must formally review an IEP at least annually for any student receiving special education services. IEPs must also be reviewed whenever any team member, including the parent, requests a review; when a student demonstrates a lack of anticipated progress; or when a student is being considered for expulsion.

Legislative Intent of the IEP

The concept of the IEP was created to serve three main functions: management, communication, and accountability. These functions are described as follows:

1. *Management.* The IEP is primarily a planning tool designed to ensure that each student is provided with special education and related services appropriate for his or her special needs in the least restrictive environment.
2. *Communication.* The IEP states in writing the present level of academic performance and the educational goals for the student. The IEP states the objectives (instruction and services) to meet the goals and serves as the agreement to provide the special education and related services needed.
3. *Accountability.* The IEP provides a tool to measure the students' progress on the specific goals and objectives. Additionally, it can serve as a measure to evaluate the district's programs.

Parent Involvement

As a minimum, parents must be notified in writing (in their primary language) of an IEP meeting. This notification must include the purpose, time, location, and names of the participants. Parents have the right to a meeting at a mutually agreed-on time and place. If the parents have been notified of the meeting in writing and by telephone and if they decline to attend, the IEP meeting may still be held at the scheduled time; and the IEP may be developed. If the parents do not participate, the team must document all attempts made by telephone, writing, or conference to encourage participation. The completed IEP must be sent to the parents for their review, approval, and signatures. The program may not be implemented without written consent from one or both parents or legal guardian(s).

Including the parents regularly in the implementation of the IEP is advisable. They can provide tremendous support toward the achievement of instructional goals and objectives. Additionally, parents can provide valuable recommendations during the review process. When the notice of the program planning meeting is being sent, a good practice is to include a form for the parents asking them to write down their thoughts about their child's strengths, weaknesses, and concerns and to list the short-term and long-term objectives that they would like to see accomplished. Parents can share this information at the meeting. Periodic updates are recommended on the student's progress toward the goals and objectives and the student's experience with adaptive strategies.

Content of the IEP

The IEP must state the student's present levels of performance, the educational goals and objectives for that student, and the educational program and related services provided. When a student is sixteen years old, a plan for transition from school to work must be included as part of the IEP. If the child requires assistive technology, appropriate goals and objectives using such technology should be included.

Present Levels of Performance

Present levels of performance describes the effect of the student's disability on the student's academic performance. This information is obtained from assessment but is not limited to standardized measures alone. Other assessment activities may be particularly useful for students suspected of having dyslexia, attention deficit disorder, or related disorders. For these students accurate determination of the present level of academic performance can prove difficult. Nonstandardized measures, such as work samples, classroom observation, and information from parents, may be used to help assess the functional level of a student's performance.

Goals and Objectives

Special education services are meant to help the student succeed in the general education curriculum. Therefore, educational goals should be written to reflect this expectation. Goals describe what the student can reasonably be expected to accomplish within a year. They should be stated in general terms and should describe the anticipated accomplishments in the areas of need.

Goals should not be directed toward a student's attaining skills that are below the grade level for the curriculum. Rather, they should reflect the development of skills and strategies that will help the student to have access to the concepts or themes that are presented at his or her particular grade level. Although students have not mastered a particular skill, they should still not be prevented from exposure to higher-level concepts because supplemental materials and aids may be used to help students master such concepts. For example, students should not work exclusively on multiplication facts as their goal for achievement in mathematics when they are in the upper grades. The reason is that the universal use of calculators makes knowing whether to multiply or divide and why more important than doing the actual computation.

Objectives (instructional steps between the level of performance and the goal) measure a student's progress toward the attainment of the goal. They must have a time line for completion and criteria to judge a student's success that are oriented toward the student rather than the district. A direct relationship must exist between the student's present levels of performance and the goals and the objectives.

"For individuals whose primary language is other than English, linguistically appropriate goals, objectives, programs, and services" are mandated by *Education Code* Section 56345(b)(4).

Specific Instruction and Frequency of Service

The IEP must specify the special educational program and related services that will be provided and the amount of time committed. The IEP team members should determine those aspects of the plan after they have developed the goals and objectives. At that time the team can best decide the time and frequency of service needed to help a student meet his or her goals and objectives in the least restrictive environment.

Least Restrictive Environment

The least restrictive environment (LRE) promotes the maximum interaction between students with disabilities and the general education population and provides the most appropriate education for those students. To accomplish these purposes, special education must provide a full continuum of options for students with disabilities. All services as agreed to on the IEP are provided free to the parent, within the context of the LRE. The options include, but are not limited to, the following:

1. Education in the general education classroom with consultative or collaborative support from special education services
2. Small-group, individualized direct instruction for part or all of the school day
3. Education at a special school at public expense if the student cannot succeed in the public schools even with the use of supplementary aids and services

Services are determined by student need rather than by state or local mandate or availability. The amount of time that a student spends in the general education program must be stated in the IEP. Related services, such as transportation and counseling, must also be provided at public expense if the team determines that these services are needed to meet the educational goals of the IEP.

During the IEP meeting it should be determined whether the student's level of performance would allow him or her to exit from the current program option into a less restrictive option. If the student can make the transition, exit criteria should be developed; and a plan for facilitating the transition between program options should also be developed.

Signatures of Participants

A listing of the names, positions, and signatures of the IEP team members who attended the meeting must appear on the IEP form as well as the date of the meeting. If the parents agree to the plan, their signatures consenting to the IEP must also appear. Parents are allowed to take the IEP form home to consider the assessment information and the plan before they sign, but no one is legally able to sign unless he or she attended the actual meeting. No services may be delivered until the parents have given their written consent on the IEP.

> **Numerous requirements for the IEP are not covered in the preceding section. For complete requirements readers should refer to federal and state laws and regulations.**

Questions and Answers

What happens if a parent or the school district refuses to give consent to the IEP?

If a parent or the school district disagrees on any component of the IEP, the district must implement the parts that can be agreed on so as not to delay the provision of instruction and services to the student. The items in the IEP that cannot be agreed to, however, become the basis for a due-process hearing. If there is disagreement about the placement option, the student must remain in the current placement pending the outcome of a due-process hearing. The procedures are described in *Education Code* Section 56501. Normally, the IEP decision is reached by consensus. If a team member other than the parent does not agree with the team's decision, then he or she may write a dissenting opinion.

Is a student still eligible for special education services if he or she moves to another school district?

Yes. The provision of special education services is guaranteed under federal law. The student must be immediately enrolled in a comparable special education program when the new school district receives verification that the student is entitled to those services. The services must be provided for a period not to exceed 30 days. Before the 30-day period expires, the IEP team must meet to make final recommendations. When the student enrolls, parents are advised to give a copy of the current IEP to the new school district.

May students receive accommodations for their disabilities if they no longer are eligible for special education services?

Students with disabilities may continue to receive reasonable accommodations in their educational programs, even if they are no longer served by special education. These rights to reasonable accommodation are guaranteed under the Americans with Disabilities Act (ADA) and Section 504 of the Rehabilitation Act of 1973 (and subsequent amendments). The ADA prohibits schools and employers from discriminating against any individual who has a physical or mental impairment that substantially limits a major life activity (including learning). The ADA also applies to any individual with a history of a handicap. Therefore, parents should keep copies of former IEPs in order to verify that their child has been considered as having a disability; document that accommodations have been provided (such as preferential seating or untimed tests); and identify strategies that have facilitated their child's educational success.

How are the time lines for referral and assessment affected by year-round scheduling?

For students who are in year-round schools, the time lines stop when the students go on vacation and start again when the students return. However, the time lines are not affected when school personnel take vacations at different times than their students.

What if the parents believe that the services agreed to in the IEP are not being provided?

The parents should request a new IEP team meeting to review the agreed-on services with team members to determine whether a misunderstanding has occurred or whether a new IEP is needed. If the parents are not satisfied, then they should notify their school superintendent, in writing, about the nature of their complaint. Some complaints may be filed with the Department of Education (see *CCR, Title 5, Education,* Section 4650). Any person, including the parent, has the right to appeal a formal written complaint with the State Superintendent of Public Instruction at the California Department of Education. Within 30 days the Department will attempt to mediate. If mediation fails or if either party waives mediation, an investigation will take place. Within 60 days the written report will list the Department's findings of facts, conclusions, and required actions, if applicable, and the time line for corrective action.

What can I do if my child is not eligible for special education services, but I still believe that he or she learns differently?

If the IEP team has determined that your child is not eligible for services, but he or she continues to perform below expectations in school, a plan should be developed to determine how your child can best be helped within a general education program. This plan can often be developed by the IEP team with the help of the school-site administrator. Additionally, the ADA requires that school districts and employers not discriminate against children who have a history of a handicapping condition or have been perceived as having a handicapping condition. You may wish to contact the special education administrator or the coordinator for ADA and Section 504 of the Rehabilitation Act of 1973 in your school district to help determine with you an appropriate way to address your child's educational needs.

How does a student exit from special education services?

Specific criteria for exiting a program are not mandated as are criteria for eligibility. When the individual needs of a student can best be met in a regular education classroom, an IEP meeting should be conducted. General and special education personnel should be included to facilitate the change in placement. The teacher receiving the student should be included as part of the IEP team.

The four situations that result in a student's exiting from special education services are as follows:

1. The student graduates.
2. The parent or student requests an exit from the program.
3. The student no longer meets the criteria for eligibility.
4. The IEP team believes that the transition to general education has been successful and that special education services are no longer necessary.

This chapter has described the concept and uses of an IEP, along with the role of an IEP team. Chapter VI describes the continuum of educational program options and methods to deliver special education services to students with an IEP. Schoolwide strategies for addressing the needs of students with differing approaches to learning are also discussed.

CHAPTER VI

Service Delivery Models and Strategies for School Sites

A *continuum of program options and methods and strategies for school sites exists to deliver special education services to students eligible for an individualized education program. The selection of program options should be determined by the IEP team from the assessed needs of the individual student. The purpose of this chapter is to inform school staff and parents about the continuum of program options and methods and the strategies for school sites to deliver special education services.*

Content and Organization

The chapter is divided into four sections: (1) background information on the continuum of service delivery models, including descriptions of the program options; (2) instruction within a variety of resource specialist program models; (3) a discussion and descriptions of strategies for school sites; and (4) answers to commonly asked questions. The first section provides an overview of the philosophy of the continuum of program options and stresses the need to select an option based on the needs of each student eligible for an IEP. It describes the six program options: general education programs; resource specialist programs; designated instruction and services; special classes and centers; nonpublic, nonsectarian school services; and state special schools. The second section contains descriptions of the variety of models for providing the services of a resource specialist: traditional direct service model, classroom intervention model, departmentalized model for students in secondary schools, consultative/collaborative model, and school-based coordinated programs model. The third section contains descriptions of ten strategies for school sites: school restructuring; Every Student Succeeds, a statewide program; the School-Based Coordinated Programs Act; student study team; consultation/collaboration; peer coaching; collaborative in-service training; schoolwide incentives; cross-age tutoring and peer tutoring; and articulation between school levels. The final section provides answers to commonly asked questions about the delivery of services to students with IEPs.

Continuum of Program Options

According to *Education Code* Section 56360, "each district, special education local plan area, or county office shall ensure that a full continuum of placement options is

101

available to meet the needs of individuals with exceptional needs for special education and related services." These options are listed as follows:

1. General education (including other categorical programs)
2. Resource specialist programs
3. Designated instruction and services
4. Special classes and centers
5. Nonpublic, nonsectarian schools or agencies or both
6. State special schools

Students eligible for special education services may receive service through any one or a combination of these options that are the most appropriate for meeting their educational goals and objectives.

General Education Programs

General education programs are offered to all students at the school without regard to any eligibility criteria. Students who are in general education programs may also be eligible for categorical programs, such as special education, bilingual education, migrant education, and other programs designed to support students in achieving an education. The current trend is toward providing special services to support the general education program and reduce the amount of time a student is removed from the general education classroom. All students should have access to the core curriculum, with assistance as needed, to maintain a satisfactory level of achievement. Only a few students will have conditions requiring that they be educated away from general education programs.

Resource Specialist Programs

Resource specialist programs are under the direction of a resource specialist who can provide instruction aligned with the core curriculum, information, assistance, consultation, resource information and material, and coordination of special education services for individuals with exceptional needs. Students who receive services from this program must be simultaneously enrolled in general education classes for the majority of the school day.

Designated Instruction and Services

Designated instruction and services should be under the direction of appropriately trained personnel and may include language and speech development and remediation, audiological services, instruction for orientation and mobility, instruction in the home or hospital, adapted physical education, physical and occupational therapy, vision services, specialized driver training instruction, counseling and guidance, psychological services other than assessment, parent counseling and training, health and nursing services, social worker services, specially designed vocational education and career development, and recreation services.

Special Classes and Centers

Special classes and centers provide instructional settings for students when the nature or severity of the disability prevents their participation in the regular school program for the majority of a school day. Students placed in these settings have the right to participate in activities with nondisabled peers as appropriate, including meals and recess periods. The classes generally are set up to approximate a general education classroom, with small class sizes and specialized instruction available to each of the students. The IEP team must document its rationale for placing a pupil in a program in other than the school and classroom that the pupil would otherwise attend if he or she did not have a disability. The documentation must indicate why the pupil's disability prevents the pupil's needs from being met in a less restrictive environment, even with the use of supplementary aids and services (see the *California Code of Regulations, Title 5, Education*, Section 3042 [b]).

Nonpublic, Nonsectarian School Services

Nonpublic, nonsectarian school services are provided to students whose needs cannot be met through the public school system. The students may be provided an education in a private school setting at public expense.

State Special Schools

State special schools serve students for whom no appropriate placement is available in the local plan area. Three state special schools in California serve students whose primary disability is deafness or blindness.

Three diagnostic centers are also operated by the California Department of Education to serve as a resource to local educational agencies (LEAs). They provide a continuum of assessment services for students with special needs, ranging from field-based assistance to transdisciplinary assessments at each center. All assessments are designed to assist IEP teams in determining curricula, instructional strategies, and program options for students. The diagnostic centers also provide LEAs with a variety of training services for staff involved with student programming issues.

Providing Instruction Within the Resource Specialist Option

The majority of California students with learning disabilities are assigned to the resource specialist program and may receive instruction in a variety of ways. Resource specialists and other specialists, such as school psychologists and speech and language therapists, may combine one or more of the approaches described in the next section when they design intervention strategies to meet the needs of students assigned to their programs. In all approaches the caseload of the full-time resource specialist is limited to 28 students unless a waiver from the State Board of Education has been obtained.

Traditional Direct Service Model

In this model the resource specialist is responsible for screening, instructional assessment, assisting in the development of the IEP, and direct service delivery (pull-out) to students individually and in small groups (see the Glossary for a definition of *pull-out*). The size of groups varies according to the severity of the disabilities of the students in the caseload. Effort is made to minimize the disruption to the students' participation in core curriculum activities in the general education classroom. Students receive individualized instruction on strategies and skills necessary for learning the core curriculum of their grade level. Frequency of service varies and must be stated on the IEP according to the student's needs.

In addition to the services described previously, the resource specialist collaborates with general classroom teachers and in-service training programs for the teacher and parent.

Classroom Intervention Model

In this model the classroom teacher and the resource specialist provide instruction collaboratively. The following are examples of collaborative instructional activities: (1) the two teachers instruct side-by-side; (2) the resource specialist develops and models alternative teaching strategies for learning disabled students; and (3) the resource specialist provides the classroom teacher with modified materials, lesson plans, and tests. In this model the resource specialist may also work with curriculum development, staff development, and parent training. This model is often chosen when the student's needs would best be met by less transition between two different instructional settings, when there is a sizable at-risk population in the general classroom, and when both teachers believe that the needs of the student with learning disabilities can best be met within the structure of the general classroom.

Departmentalized Model for Students in Secondary Schools

In the departmentalized model for students in secondary schools, the resource specialist teaches individuals with exceptional needs in core academic areas during selected class periods. Curriculum content is applied to both the instruction in academic content and the remediation of reading and language or mathematics. These classes usually are scheduled for one period each, five times per week. Students are scheduled into these classes by the school counselors in the same manner as that for regular classes. Students receive course credit toward junior high school and senior high school graduation requirements.

Consultative/Collaborative Model

The consultative/collaborative model is one in which the resource specialist becomes a resource person and adviser to teachers, parents, administrators, and other support personnel in the schools. The resource specialist answers questions, provides information, presents demonstrations, and facilitates access to resources. The resource specialist continues to provide instructional assessment services and advises staff on appropriate instructional programs and effective strategies for teaching students with learning disabilities. This model differs from the classroom intervention model because the general education teacher provides the direct instruction to the student on the basis of the goals and objectives within the IEP.

School-Based Coordinated Programs Model

In 1981 the Legislature enacted the School-Based Coordinated Programs (SBCP) Act to enable schools to have flexible use of certain categorical resources. This flexibility can help ensure that all students, including those with disabilities, can acquire the knowledge, understanding, and skills of the district's core curriculum through the coordination of one or more categorically funded programs at the school site. Each site that participates in this program must have a plan, approved by the school site council and the school district governing board, detailing the ways in which students who are eligible for the different categorical programs will receive services. If state special education funds are included in the SBCP plan, the district must still comply with all federal regulations pertaining to special education.

Strategies for School Sites

Schools committed to educating all children will often collaborate on schoolwide strategies for addressing the needs of students with differing approaches to learning. These strategies can effectively meet the needs of diverse populations and promote schoolwide effectiveness. This section provides information about several different, successful approaches. Schools can examine the approaches and consider using or adapting those that seem the most practical and have the most promise for that particular school. The approaches described are school restructuring; Every Student Succeeds, a statewide program; the School-Based Coordinated Programs Act; student study team; consultation/collaboration; peer coaching; collaborative in-service training; schoolwide incentives; cross-age tutoring and peer tutoring; and articulation between school levels.

Background of Strategies for School Sites

In any general education classroom, students' levels of interest, skills, and abilities vary. All teachers must deal with individual learning needs, whether or not the needs have been formally diagnosed. Schools that effectively serve a wide range of students are committed to the belief that all students can and should succeed in the school's basic academic (core) curriculum. Once a local school's staff, parents, administration, and community agree on and support this philosophy, it should become the foundation for action. Researchers have identified a number of essential practices that a school community can engage in to support the success of all students. The school community should provide the following:

1. Opportunities for active learning so that students become totally involved and able to demonstrate their knowledge and skills
2. Expectations for individualized performance that take individual differences into account
3. Varied learning environments that avoid a single, standard mode of instruction
4. Repertoires of learning strategies and study skills that emphasize reflective thought and systematic progress toward the goal of independent learning
5. Encouragement and incentives to pursue academic and occupational goals regardless of a student's native language, ethnic background, gender, or disability
6. Opportunities to demonstrate understanding through the use of authentic methods of assessment, such as the use of portfolios and projects

The essential practices listed previously are components of the strategies for school sites described in the section that follows.

School Restructuring

Many statewide restructuring efforts are under way to meet the needs of an increasingly varied population and to address the issues of students' postgraduation outcomes and efficient funding of education. Efforts to restructure schools are generally undertaken to change the way that students receive instruction or services. As the administrative and instructional leader, the site principal plays an important role in improving the local school's services to students. The principal helps staff members define the school's needs and recommend improvements in curriculum and instruction. These changes may include new roles for a school's personnel and parents. Enriched subject-matter offerings and diverse instructional approaches may be included. Planning for those changes is crucial. Programs unique to a school's particular site may be developed to accelerate the achievement for students performing below their potential.

Every Student Succeeds

Every Student Succeeds (ESS) is a statewide program to ensure success for students at risk. The six elements in the ESS initiative can serve as a conceptual framework for ensuring the success of students who are considered at risk for school failure. The elements are listed as follows:

1. *Success for every student in learning a rich core curriculum. Every* student is successful in learning the district-adopted curriculum based on the state frameworks.
2. *A preventive approach.* Students at risk of school failure should be identified early. Schools need to intervene to ensure that those students continue to have successful educational experiences by building on their strengths through enrichment.
3. *Integrated total program for each student.* Schools should integrate all core and supplementary services for each student to ensure that students have the most effective, comprehensive, and coherent educational experience possible. The services include those provided by personnel (from within and outside the school) from categorical programs, special education, and health and social services. The services should include the active support and involvement of parents and community members.
4. *Effective staff development.* All school staff should receive training that covers the state curriculum frameworks, curriculum projects, assessment strategies, models from current research on effective schools, techniques for identifying and assessing students' learning styles, and motivational strategies for increasing the participation of less-motivated students.
5. *Planning, implementing, and evaluating the total school program.* School systems should establish processes and structures for planning, implementing, and evaluating initiatives that dramatically improve the school's effect on the academic, psychological, and social outcomes of its students at risk, both individually and collectively.

6. *Whatever else is needed for every student to succeed.* Schools should do whatever they can legally, professionally, and ethically to help each student to succeed academically, psychologically, and socially.

School-Based Coordinated Programs Act

In 1981 the Legislature passed the School-Based Coordinated Programs (SBCP) Act, which allows local schools flexible use of certain funding from special programs for specific populations of students; for example, low socioeconomic-level, bilingual, or low-achieving students. Such programs are called categorical programs. Becoming an SBCP school enables the staff members to focus on students rather than on sources of funding. Participation in the program requires a written plan that describes how the school will meet all students' educational needs. In the past schools would often use individual categorical funding sources to purchase the services of a remedial reading or mathematics teacher, who was allowed to work only with those students who were eligible to participate in that particular program. Under SBCP the staff members are able to coordinate and plan instructional delivery systems more efficiently for students who may have a combination of special needs. Thus, a teacher with a particular expertise might be assigned to work with a student who needs that skill, even though the teacher is not paid directly by the categorical funding source. Consequently, it is anticipated that as general education teachers and specialists begin to work cooperatively under this program, they will be able to identify new ways to provide supportive services in the general education classroom as well as through coordinated pull-out activities (see the Glossary for a definition of *pull-out activities*). Parents of students who are receiving special education services through this approach must be informed about how IEP goals and objectives will be addressed.

The School-Based Coordinated Programs Act also provides for staff development. School personnel have eight staff development days during the school year for intensive training in strategies that maximize learning. Planning how to best integrate instructional services for all students is a part of the program.

Student Study Team

As a function of general education at a school site, the student study team reviews individual student problems and plans alternative instructional strategies that can be implemented in the general classroom. The members engage in a structured problem-solving process, focusing on a student's individual needs. Membership on the team involves the parent in a collaborative effort with the classroom teachers, administration, and other resource personnel as well as with the student when appropriate.

The responsibilities of the team members are described as follows:

1. The parents, as partners in the process, should share their history (family, developmental, and health) and school concerns; provide accounts of effective and ineffective home interventions; clarify their child's past educational history; and participate in implementing strategies developed by the team.

2. The referring teacher and other staff involved with the student share information about the student's strengths and the effects of attempted interventions as well as their concerns about the student's progress.

3. The student shares information related to difficulties and interests, identifies incentives that motivate, and makes a commitment to try any solutions that are developed.

A joint action plan is developed designating alternative strategies that can be implemented in the student's home and school environments and that address the individual's instructional, social, and behavioral needs.

Personnel are assigned to implement the strategies, and time lines are designated for their completion. A follow-up date is set to determine whether the joint action plan effectively met the concerns about the student. This process can be repeated as often as necessary to ensure the student's continued success.

The relative effectiveness of interventions should be documented so that parents and current as well as future teachers have this information for continuing reference. In addition, parents should also maintain their own records, which may include family history and interventions and their relative effectiveness as well as records of informal and formal meetings. If the child should be referred for special education or other categorical programs and not qualify, the student study team should reconvene to examine any new information gathered from the assessment and develop other alternatives.

Consultation/Collaboration

Teachers can share with experts from other disciplines in order to collaborate on students' needs. School psychologists and other professionals who have been trained in consultation can work with teachers to help define the focus of concern, provide alternative perspectives on student development, and solve problems.

Peer Coaching

Peer coaching is a model in which teachers help each other improve instructional effectiveness. This model will succeed if the teacher and the peer coach can work cooperatively. Appropriate training and release time must be provided for teachers to coach each other effectively. Therefore, this activity is best done with the teacher choosing the coach with whom he or she most prefers to work.

In this model the coach observes the teacher during an instructional activity. After the lesson the coach and teacher identify the strengths of the lesson and the most effective teaching techniques. The coach then invites the teacher to discuss aspects of the lesson that could have been done differently or that did not go as well as the teacher had hoped with a particular student or group of students. The coach works with the teacher to identify new strategies for instructing those students on the same content. The teacher then tries one of the strategies and works with the coach in follow-up sessions for feedback.

Collaborative In-service Training

Every school district must provide a program of continuing education for its teachers. Most school districts provide at least one in-service training day per year and numerous staff meetings devoted to professional growth. Schools that participate in the School-Based Coordinated Program may take up to eight full days for staff development. Teachers should collaboratively determine specific topics for in-service training. Because many workshops are relevant to all teachers, including diagnostic teaching, learning styles, behavior management, and affective education, general and special educators should work together sharing expertise and different perspectives in these areas.

Schoolwide Incentives

School staff should consider designing flexible programs that honor student achievement. Such programs allow for individualization yet recognize the efforts of students with learning difficulties. For example, elementary school students who read 1,000 pages might be rewarded with membership in the Thousand Page Club; but the difficulty of the reading level may be adjusted for individuals.

Schoolwide programs may also honor student achievement in areas other than academic subjects. Students with learning difficulties may demonstrate strengths in the fine arts, athletics, school attendance, and behavior. Recognition of achievement in these areas may help increase students' sense of self-worth and belonging to the school community—feelings that will increase their ability to tackle the difficult task of academic learning.

Cross-age Tutoring and Peer Tutoring

In many classrooms an academically talented student is asked to help the student who is having difficulties. When students are in different grade levels, this activity is called *cross-age tutoring;* for example, a fifth-grade student tutors one in the first grade. This activity is called *peer tutoring* when both students are in the same grade. Although this approach provides short-term assistance for some students, the long-term effect on the retention of new learning by struggling students is uncertain. This activity may not be effective with students with dyslexia.

Cross-age tutoring and peer tutoring are beneficial when tutors have been trained in effective ways to prepare materials, give cues, and reinforce correct responses. If students practice through modeling and role-playing, training sessions can be completed in two or three half-hour sessions. Training can be done by class or in small groups by the general classroom teacher.

Articulation Between School Levels

Changes between levels (that is, between elementary school and middle school or junior high school and between middle school or junior high school and senior high school) are difficult for most students; but those changes are especially trying for the child who has been experiencing difficulties in school. School districts must plan for the transition of students. Records of successful contact and interventions with the parents should be passed on *systematically* to the new school. The student's final report card may be one way to transfer that information. Another way would be to include the information in the student's cumulative file, a source of records to which teachers and school counselors have access. Parents should also have a copy of the information and maintain it as a part of their records so that new teachers will have essential records as the student progresses through the grades. In this way students' needs can be quickly met in the new environment and the probability of failure lessened.

Questions and Answers

When enrollment in a special education program in the school district is full, may students be put on a waiting list?

Waiting lists for services are legal only for children from birth to two years of age for whom the provision of special education services is permissive (as of the date this publication was prepared). Although the special education local plan area (SELPA) is required to provide the full continuum of program options, some options may not be available at every school site.

What is the role of the IEP team in identifying the learning style of the student and matching it with the teaching styles of school personnel?

The IEP team may determine a student's learning style during the assessment process. The team may make a recommendation to the appropriate school administrator regarding the type of teaching style that would best accommodate that student's needs. However, no single "brand name" teaching methodology or program can be required.

Is any model better than others?

One model should not be selected by a site or the district because the options, interventions, or strategies depend on the students' needs. Flexibility of service options is essential. The needs of the student and the IEP determine the service delivery mode.

Conclusion

The conclusion contains a discussion of the background of children's difficulties with learning and performance. To help children more effectively, readers of this document are encouraged to explore the complexities of such difficulties.

Background of Difficulties with Children's Learning and Performance

For many years parents and teachers have been concerned about children who seem as if they should be doing better in school. Over the years a number of labels have been applied to these children, such as learning-disabled, neurologically handicapped, brain-injured, hyperactive, attention deficient, dyslexic, dysgraphic, or learning-disordered. A variety of philosophical principles have been promoted by thinkers, researchers, and practitioners from education, psychology, and medicine. The debates on what constitutes a learning disability have gone on for years and show few signs of abating. The same statement can be applied to the condition known as dyslexia.

Along with each philosophical principle has come a set of procedures to ameliorate children's learning difficulties. A variety of teaching techniques, teaching materials, psychological counseling, psychotherapy, physical exercises, diets, medications, relaxation treatments, play therapy, art therapy, music therapy, and computer-aided instruction have been developed, prescribed, and tried with children. Children have been taught by college student tutors; by experienced teachers in small-, medium-, and large-size classes; and by teachers trained in special techniques of instruction in reading. The effects of the treatments have been mixed. Some children benefited; others did not. Because the children have such varied patterns of individual characteristics, it has been almost impossible to examine the research and come to any definite conclusion about what works. What can a parent and teacher do? How can the child be helped to learn and perform?

Recent research studies have emphasized the variety of ways in which children receive information, process it, and show that they have learned it and can apply it. This approach has been termed the "differing learning abilities" approach in contrast to the "learning disability" approach. Even before the emphasis on the differing learning abilities approach, the concept of early observation of children and early intervention was used to prevent, as much as is possible, failure in school.

Early observation builds on the daily opportunities teachers and parents have to notice the child's actions in a variety of situations: alone, in small groups, in a classroom, in the school hall, on the playground, on a school bus, at home, in the neighborhood, at different times during the day, and in different activities. What does the child seem to pay attention to? What details seem to interest him or her? Which activities does the child seem to enjoy and perhaps seek out? Which activities does the child seem to dislike or perhaps to avoid? These situations give a fairly well-rounded picture of the child from observers familiar with him or her.

Observation should also include watching and listening to the child. What kinds of details does the child pick out; for example, when viewing a school building? Doors? A pattern of windows? Colors? Given an opportunity to ask questions, what kinds of questions does the child ask? *Yes-no* questions? *When* questions? *Why* questions? *How* questions? The expert observer can make tentative deductions about a child's pattern of action. Although a parent may perhaps be a professionally untrained observer, a parent is certainly an expert observer of his or her child. Together, the teacher and parent can pool their observations and build a more complete "picture" of the child.

Early intervention is not aimed at "curing" the problem. Rather, early intervention is aimed at finding out *how* a child learns and *how* the child can show what he or she has learned. With that individualized information, the teacher can teach and test; the child can learn, perform, and achieve; and the parents can help the child at home in a consistent way.

Complexity of Learning and Performance Difficulties

Assessing the difference between academic underachievement and a learning disability or an attention deficit problem is difficult, as was discussed in Chapter IV. Further, it must be acknowledged that without expert assistance, teachers and parents cannot help all children, no matter how hard they (and the children) try. Some children do not seem to benefit from adaptations in the general classroom instruction or in modes of performance. As was discussed in Part Two, these children may be referred for assessment and, with the agreement of their parents, are assessed. If a child is identified as an individual with exceptional needs, he or she receives special education services to help overcome the effects of the disability. Some terms commonly used to describe some of the disabilities are:

- Specific learning disabilities
- Dyslexia
- Attention deficit disorder
- Attention deficit hyperactivity disorder

The terms refer *not* to children but to a group or constellation of conditions. At times the conditions occur in conjunction with other conditions, such as behavioral disorders, emotional disorders, or other health impairments in such combinations as to make them difficult to untangle.

Other children who do not seem to have benefited from adaptations may be referred for assessment for possible needs for special education services but are found to be ineligible for such services. These children remain in their general classrooms, and their teachers can use the assessment information and the recommendations of the assessment team to make further adaptations.

General classrooms have always had students with a broad range of learning styles and behaviors that different teachers were accustomed to in varying degrees. The changing school population, with an increasing diversity of backgrounds, languages, and cultures, poses new challenges to educators. Two recent developments, least restrictive environment and inclusion, are affecting the practice of labeling a child as a "child with a disability." Educators are placing an increased importance on meeting students' needs through the least restrictive environment. Parents, persons with disabilities, and the community are placing increasing emphasis on the inclusion of children with disabilities in general classes. The combination of these two developments is making less advisable the practice of labeling a child as "a child with a disability" in order to get special education services.

Looking into the future, researchers are making progress in understanding the variety of ways the human mind works. For example, advances in medical science and technology may assist in discovering how a particular person receives and processes incoming information. One such advance is called neuroimaging. Another example is the knowledge of interactions among pharmaceutical drugs in the developing and adult brain. Sometimes, this field of knowledge is called psychopharmacology. This knowledge might help us understand why certain medications seem to work with one child, have unfortunate side effects with another, and have no positive effect for yet another. As in teaching a child with learning or performance difficulties, medical science professionals know that no standard approach exists that works with everyone.

Teachers and parents cannot afford to wait for educational researchers or medical science to find the final, definitive answers for all children with learning or performance difficulties. Their responsibility to the child is to do what they can today. The child cannot wait. Waiting will only increase the difficulties and add to the child's problems. He or she will fall further behind. The child knows what is happening and nearly always is not happy about falling behind. How much better it is to help the children know their own strengths and capitalize on their success. Then success in school can lead more directly to success in adult life.

Users of this document who wish more information on specific learning disabilities, dyslexia, attention deficits, or attention deficit hyperactivity are encouraged to look into the professional literature or get in touch with persons who are knowledgeable in the field. A brief list of specialized references that may be available from a local college library follows. In addition, a list of selected references to provide additional information about the topics discussed in each chapter appears in the last part of this publication.

Selected References

The Assessment of Learning Disabilities, Preschool Through Adulthood. Edited by Larry B. Silver. Austin, Tex.: PRO-ED, 1989.

Ayres, A. Jean. *Sensory Integration and Learning Disorders.* Los Angeles: Western Psychological Services, 1973.

Children with ADD: A Shared Responsibility. Reston, Va.: Council for Exceptional Children, 1992.

Cohen, Libby G. *Children with Exceptional Needs in Regular Classrooms.* Washington, D.C.: National Education Association, 1992.

Dane, Elizabeth. *Painful Passages: Working with Children with Learning Disabilities.* Washington, D.C.: National Association of Social Workers, 1990.

Gaddes, William H. *Learning Disabilities and Brain Function* (Second edition). New York: Springer-Verlag, Inc., 1992.

Gadow, Kenneth D. *Children on Medication.* Vol. 1: *Hyperactivity Learning Disabilities and Mental Retardation.* Austin, Tex.: PRO-ED, 1986.

Gallico, Robin P., and others. *Emotional and Behavioral Problems in Children with Learning Disabilities.* San Diego: Singular Publishing Group, Inc., 1991.

Genetics and Learning Disabilities. Edited by Shelly D. Smith. Austin, Tex.: College Hill Press, Inc., 1986.

Hooper, Stephen R., and W. G. Willis. *Learning Disability Subtyping: Neuropsychological Foundations, Conceptual Models, and Issues in Clinical Differentiation.* New York: Springer-Verlag, Inc., 1988.

Hosler, Virginia N., and Jack L. Fadely. *Learning Disabled Children Who Succeed.* Springfield, Ill.: Charles C. Thomas Publishers, 1989.

Hynd, George W., and others. "Learning Disabilities and Presumed Central Nervous System Dysfunction," *Learning Disability Quarterly,* Vol. 14, No. 4 (fall, 1991), 283–96.

Johnston, Robert B. *Attention Deficits, Learning Disabilities, and Ritalin: A Practical Guide* (Second edition). San Diego: Singular Publishing Group, Inc., 1991.

King, Warren L., and Jane Jarrow. *Testing Accommodations for Students with Disabilities.* Columbus, Ohio: Association on Handicapped Student Services Programs in Postsecondary Education, 1990.

Kronick, Doreen. *New Approaches to Learning Disabilities: Cognitive, Metacognitive, and Holistic.* Philadelphia: Grune and Stratton, W. B. Saunders Company, Harcourt Brace Jovanovich, Inc., 1988.

Learning Disabilities: Theoretical and Research Issues. Proceedings of the 1988 Conference of the International Association for Research in Learning Disabilities. Edited by H. Lee Swanson and Barbara Keogh. Hillsdale, N.J.: Lawrence Erlbaum Associates, Inc., 1990.

Liberman I. Y., and A. M. Liberman. "Whole Language Versus Code Emaphsis: Underlying Assumptions and Their Implications for Reading," *Annals of Dyslexia,* Vol. 40, (1990), 51–76.

Orton, Samuel T. *Reading, Writing, and Speech Problems in Children and Selected Papers.* 1937. Reprint. Austin, Tex.: PRO-ED, 1989.

Pennington, Bruce F. *Diagnosing Learning Disorders: A Neuropsychological Framework.* New York: Guilford Press, 1991.

Rourke, Byron P., and Darren R. Fuerst. *Learning Disabilities and Psychosocial Functioning: A Neuropsychological Perspective.* New York: Guilford Press, 1991.

Silver, Archie A., and Rose A. Hagin. *Disorders of Learning in Childhood.* New York: John Wiley and Sons, Inc., 1990.

Trapani, Catherine. *Transition Goals for Adolescents with Learning Disabilities.* Austin, Tex.: PRO-ED, 1990.

Whitmore, Joanne Rand, and C. June Maker. *Intellectual Giftedness in Disabled Persons.* Austin, Tex.: PRO-ED, 1985. (Out of print)

APPENDIX A

Agencies, Groups, and Organizations

T his list of resources shows where help may be obtained for persons with learning disabilities. Public agencies, advocacy groups, state and national organizations, and professional groups are represented.

Public Agencies

Special Education Division
California Department of Education
721 Capitol Mall
P.O. Box 944272
Sacramento, CA 95844-2720
(916) 445-4613; FAX: (916) 327-3516

Department of Rehabilitation
830 K Street
Sacramento, CA 95814
(916) 445-8638
ADA Implementation Section
(916) 322-0251

Office for Civil Rights, Region IX
U.S. Department of Health and Human
    Services
50 United Nations Plaza, Room 322
San Francisco, CA 94102
(415) 556-7000; TTY (415) 556-6806

Advocacy Groups

Community Alliance on Special Education
1031 Franklin Street, B5
San Francisco, CA 94109
(415) 928-2273

Disability Rights Education and Defense
    Fund, Inc. (DREDF)
2212 Sixth Street
Berkeley, CA 94710
(510) 644-2555

Parents Helping Parents
535 Race Street, Suite 220
San Jose, CA 95126
(408) 288-5010

Protection and Advocacy, Inc.
100 Howe Avenue, Suite 185 N
Sacramento, CA 95825
(916) 488-9950

Professional Groups

Alliance for Technology Access
1307 Solano Avenue
Albany, CA 94706
(415) 528-0747

Association of Educational Therapists
P.O. Box 946
Woodland Hills, CA 91365
(818) 788-3850

California Association for Bilingual
    Education
926 J Street, Suite 810
Sacramento, CA 95814
(916) 447-3986

California Association of Program
    Specialists
c/o Brian Ross, President
875 E. Cochran
Simi Valley, CA 93065

California Association of Resource
  Specialists
P.O. Box 7469
Citrus Heights, CA 95621-7469
(916) 448-0529

California Association of School
  Psychologists
180 El Camino Real, Suite 5
Millbrae, CA 94030
(415) 697-9672

California Speech, Language, and
  Hearing Association
825 University Avenue
Sacramento, CA 95825
(916) 921-1568

California Teachers Association
Instructional and Professional
  Development Department
1705 Murchison Drive
Burlingame, CA 94010
(415) 697-1400

State and National Organizations

Children with Attention Deficit
  Disorders (CHADD)
499 N.W. 70th Avenue, Suite 308
Plantation, FL 33317
(305) 587-3700

Council for Exceptional Children
1920 Association Drive
Reston, VA 22901
(703) 620-3660

Council for Learning Disabilities
Box 40303
Overland Park, KS 66204
(913) 492-8755

Division on Learning Disabilities
The Council for Exceptional Children
1920 Association Drive
Reston, VA 22091-1589

Learning Disabilities Association of
  America
4156 Library Road
Pittsburgh, PA 15234
(413) 341-1515

Learning Disabilities Association of
  California
655 Lewelling Boulevard
P.O. Box 365
San Leandro, CA 94579
(415) 383-5242

National Association of School
  Psychologists (NASP)
8455 Colesville Road, Suite 1000
Silver Spring, MD 20910
(301) 608-0500

National Attention Deficit Disorder
  Association
P.O. Box 488
West Newbury, MA 01985
1-800-487-2282

National Center for Learning Disabilities
318 Park Avenue, South
New York, NY 10016
(212) 545-7510

National Information Center for Children
  and Youth with Disabilities
P.O. Box 1492
Washington, DC 20013
1-800-999-5599

National Parent Network on Disabilities
1600 Prince Street, Suite 115
Alexandria, VA 22314
(703) 684-6763

Orton Dyslexia Society
Chester Building, Suite 382
8600 La Salle Road
Baltimore, MD 21204-6020
1-800-ABCD-123

Recording for the Blind
20 Roszel Road
Princeton, NJ 08540

APPENDIX B

Selected Legal Requirements

(As of January, 1994)

(Noncodified Sections)

(AB 3040 - Chapter 1501, Statutes of 1990)

SECTION 1. The Legislature hereby finds and declares all of the following:

(a) The National Institutes of Health states that 10 to 15 percent of our population have learning disabilities.

(b) In California, dyslexia is a specific language disability that often goes undetected in many children.

(c) Preservice and in-service programs for regular education and special education teachers in California need to provide more emphasis on recognizing characteristics of pupils with dyslexia and need updated teaching strategies for public school pupils with dyslexia and its related disorders.

(d) Regular education and special education teachers in California do not have state program guidelines available to them as a resource to assist them in identifying, assessing, planning, providing, evaluating, and improving educational services to pupils with dyslexia and its related disorders.

SEC. 2. (a) The Superintendent of Public Instruction shall develop program guidelines for specific learning disabilities, including dyslexia and other related disorders, for use by regular and special educators and parents to assist them in identifying, assessing, planning, providing, evaluating, and improving educational services to pupils. The program guidelines shall include characteristics typical of pupils with dyslexia and related disorders and include strategies for their remediation. The superintendent shall consult with teachers, administrators, other education professionals, medical professionals, parents, and professionals involved in the identification and treatment of specific learning disabilities, including dyslexia and other related disorders. The program guidelines shall be completed in time for use no later than the beginning of the 1992–93 academic year. Once the program guidelines are completed, the superintendent shall disseminate them, and provide technical assistance regarding their use and implementation, to parents, teachers, administrators, and faculty members in teacher training programs of institutions of higher education.

(b) The State Department of Education shall use available discretionary federal funds for the purpose of developing program guidelines as required under subdivision (a).

Education Code sections added by AB 2773, Chapter 1360, statutes of 1992, pertaining to learning disabilities

56337.5. (a) A pupil who is assessed as being dyslexic and meets eligibility criteria specified in Section 56337 and subdivision (j) of Section 3030 of *Title 5* of the *California Code of Regulations* for the federal Individuals with Disabilities Education Act (20 *U.S.C.* Sec. 1400 and following) category of specific learning disabilities is entitled to special education and related services.

(b) If a pupil who exhibits the characteristics of dyslexia or another related reading dysfunction is not found to be eligible for special education and related services pursuant to subdivision (a), the pupil's instructional program shall be provided in the regular education program.

(c) It is the intent of the Legislature that the program guidelines developed pursuant to Section 2 of Chapter 1501 of the Statutes of 1990, for specific learning disabilities, including dyslexia and other related disorders, be available for use by teachers and parents in order for them to have knowledge of the strategies that can be utilized with pupils for the remediation of the various types of specific learning disabilities.

SEC. 14. Article 2.6 (commencing with Section 56339) is added to Chapter 4 of Part 30 of the *Education Code,* to read:

Article 2.6 Attention Deficit and Hyperactivity Disorders

56339. (a) A pupil whose educational performance is adversely affected by a suspected or diagnosed attention deficit disorder or attention deficit hyperactivity disorder and demonstrates a need for special education and related services by meeting eligibility criteria specified in subdivision (f) or (i) of Section 3030 of *Title 5* of the *California Code of Regulations* or [*Education Code*] Section 56337 and subdivision (j) of Section 3030 of *Title 5* of the *California Code of Regulations* for the federal Individuals with Disabilities Education Act (20 *U.S.C.* Sec. 1400 and following) categories of "other health impairments," "serious emotional disturbance," or "specific learning disabilities," is entitled to special education and related services.

(b) If a pupil with an attention deficit disorder or attention deficit hyperactivity disorder is not found to be eligible for special education and related services pursuant to subdivision (a), the pupil's instructional program shall be provided in the regular education program.

(c) It is the intent of the Legislature that local educational agencies promote coordination between special education and regular education programs to ensure that all pupils, including those with attention deficit disorders or attention deficit hyperactivity disorders, receive appropriate instructional interventions.

(d) It is further the intent of the Legislature that regular education teachers and other personnel be trained to develop an awareness about attention deficit disorders and attention deficit hyperactivity disorders and the manifestations of those disorders, and the adaptations that can be implemented in regular education programs to address the instructional needs of pupils having these disorders.

Characteristics of Children with Attention Disorders

Each child with ADHD or ADD has a unique set of symptoms and characteristics. This handout is intended to assist you in recognizing the symptoms of attention disorders in your students. After understanding the difficulties associated with ADHD, you should be able to recognize the symptoms. If you do suspect that a student has ADHD, we urge you to encourage his family to seek professional assistance from someone thoroughly familiar with this disorder. Proper diagnosis is crucial to establishing appropriate and effective treatment interventions.

The major symptoms of ADHD originally described by the American Psychiatric Association and ones which continue to be viewed as major problems are divided into three categories. These are: (1) inattention and distractibility, (2) impulsivity, and (3) problems with activity level—either overactivity or underactivity.

Inattention and Distractibility

Almost every student with ADHD displays poor attention. It can be seen as a short attention span, inattentiveness, or an inability to concentrate. The student may miss important parts of directions or have difficulty staying on task. Spaciness, another quality of inattentiveness, is the inability of a child to notice important stimuli to which he should respond. For example, the student may have every intention of listening to the directions for the math homework. He does listen, but does not hear that it was to be done in pencil and not pen.

Another attention problem seen frequently in ADHD students is their choice of the wrong stimuli to which to respond. This student may be able to describe in detail the floral print on the teacher's dress, but she did not hear what the history homework is.

Distractibility is defined as becoming sidetracked by other stimuli which are not relevant to the task at hand. Distractions may be internal (such as the feelings of hunger) or external (the car outside, the pencil on the floor or the pictures on the wall).

The student's physiological inability to concentrate may also make it especially difficult for him to complete long tasks or ones he considers boring. His constant off-task behaviors and his avoiding settling down to work are frustrating for the teacher and student alike. As much as he wants to be successful in school, the ADHD child's physical limitations often cause him to be extremely disappointed in himself.

Indications of inattention and distractibility are:

- Short attention span
- Difficulty completing tasks
- Daydreaming
- Easily distracted
- Nicknames such as: "spacey" or "dreamer"
- Much activity but little accomplishment
- Enthusiastic beginnings but poor endings

Impulsivity

The inability to think before acting and to tolerate delay is considered by many to be the most serious and enduring problem for ADHD adolescents and adults. These children are usually not malicious—simply unthinking. Pulling Susie's pigtails, grabbing John's book, or speaking out in class often happen quickly and without negative intent. These students are also frequently disorganized and forgetful; they constantly lose assignments, books, papers or homework. Staying organized is perhaps the most difficult task for

This material appears in Edna D. Copeland and Valerie L. Love, *Attention Without Tension: A Teacher's Handbook on Attention Disorders (ADHD and ADD)* (Revised edition). Atlanta, Ga.: Resurgens Press, 1992, pp. 30–36. Copyright © 1990 by Edna D. Copeland. Reprinted by permission of the author. For more information one may contact Resurgens Press, Inc., 1770 Old Spring House Lane, Suite 111, Atlanta, GA 30338; telephone 1-800-526-5952.

ADHD students, in spite of valiant attempts to *get it all together.*

Indications of impulsivity are:

- Excitability
- Low frustration tolerance
- Acting before thinking
- Disorganization
- Poor planning ability
- Excessive shifting from one activity to another
- Difficulty in group situations which require patience and taking turns
- Requiring much supervision
- Constantly in trouble for inappropriate behavior

Activity Level Problems

Children with ADHD vary in their activity level, ranging from underactive and lethargic to overactive and hyperactive. *Not all children with attention disorders are hyperactive.* In fact, *most* are not. The underactive child, however, is often not recognized and, therefore, is least likely to receive help. He is generally not impulsive and does not display excessive motor activity. He does, however, have difficulty paying attention and may appear confused and depressed. He is often viewed as being *lazy, disinterested, or having a poor attitude.* Both parents and teachers are often frustrated with this student because of poor performance on all tasks requiring discipline, planning and organization.

The hyperactive child, by contrast, appears to be in constant motion. He may drum his fingers, interrupt in class, pick on his classmates or talk constantly. He has great difficulty sitting in his seat and often appears to be *nervous.* In unusual settings, or in a one-to-one situation, however, these students are frequently able to respond like other children at least for a while. Research has shown that the more restrictive the environment and the more concentration required, the more likely it is that restless and off-task behavior will occur.

Indications of activity-level problems are:

Overactivity/Hyperactivity

- Restlessness—either fidgetiness or being constantly on the go
- Diminished need for sleep
- Excessive talking
- Excessive running, jumping and climbing
- Motor restlessness during sleep; kicking covers off—moving around constantly
- Difficulty staying seated at meals, in class, etc.; often walks around classroom

Underactivity

- Lethargy
- Daydreaming or spaciness
- Failure to complete tasks
- Inattention
- Poor leadership ability
- Difficulty in learning and performing

While the preceding characteristics of inattention, impulsivity and activity-level problems are the most common symptoms of ADHD, the following characteristics are also seen frequently in students with ADHD.

Noncompliance

ADHD students frequently do not mind in class and do not behave in socially-acceptable ways when relating to fellow classmates. Noncompliance is sometimes due to a lack of training in self-control and problem solving. However, experts believe that, even with the best of training in these areas, some children will not develop these behaviors unless they are neurologically mature enough to acquire the language skills necessary to develop cognitive alternatives.

Indications of noncompliance are:

- Does not mind
- Is argumentative
- Disregards socially-accepted behavioral expectations
- *Forgets*—more deeds of omission than commission

Attention-Getting Behavior

The ADHD child's need to be noticed at all times is perhaps the most frustrating characteristic for teachers to deal with in the classroom. His need for attention appears insatiable. He may blurt out questions, pick on the other children, use bad language or interrupt frequently. Under conditions of increased competition, attention-getting behavior accelerates even more. Just notice when the principal drops by!

Indications of attention-getting behavior are:

- Frequently needs to be the center of attention
- Constantly asks questions or interrupts
- Engages in bad language or negative behavior to gain attention
- Irritates and annoys siblings, peers and adults
- Is the *class clown*

Immaturity

Emotional, physical, neurological and social immaturity are typically present in the ADHD child. This becomes especially evident as expected tasks, such as learning cursive writing, for example, appear incredibly difficult for a student. These *late bloomers* may reach various levels of maturity six months to several years later than their classmates. For this reason, they frequently enjoy the company of younger classmates who are their neurological peers.

Indications of immaturity are:

- Much of the behavior is that of a younger child (responses are typical of children six months to two-plus years younger).
- Physical development is delayed; neurological development is delayed.
- Younger children are preferred and relationships are better.
- Emotional reactions are immature.

School Problems

Poor school performance and underachievement are close to universal problems from preschool through college. An ADHD child usually has trouble because he cannot concentrate and complete the work. Learning which does not require concentration and disciplined effort, such as vocabulary, comprehension and general information, is less affected than academic tasks which require repetition, memory and problem solving. The ADHD student's impaired ability to concentrate, to attend to what is said, and to lock information into long-term memory inhibit his acquisition of many academic skills and decrease his fund of knowledge.

Indications of school problems are:

- Underachievement in relation to ability is present (especially by third grade).
- Books, assignments, clothes and other material are lost.
- Auditory memory and auditory processing problems or visual memory and visual processing problems are present.
- Learning disabilities may coexist with the ADHD.
- Handwriting is poor.
- Written work is often described as "messy" or "sloppy."
- Assignments are often not completed.
- Academic work is performed too quickly or too slowly.

Emotional Difficulties

The emotional problems experienced by many ADHD children may be the result of physiological or psychological causes. Their frequent irritability, moodiness and quick tempers can be constant challenges in the classroom. Ongoing underachievement, criticism, failure and frustration result in low self-esteem for the majority of ADHD children. Perceiving themselves as *dumb* or *different,* they all wish for someone or something to help them.

Indications of emotional difficulties are:

- Frequent and unpredictable mood swings: happy one minute and miserable the next; or good days and bad days

- Irritability
- Underreactive to pain/insensitive to danger
- Easily overstimulated; hard to stop once "revved up"
- Low frustration tolerance; excessive emotional reaction to frustrating situations
- Temper tantrums, angry outbursts
- Moodiness/lack of energy
- Low self-esteem

Poor Peer Relations

Problems with peers often begin in preschool, especially for the hyperactive child. Aggression and teasing are seen most frequently in this age group, while bossiness, difficulty taking turns and impulsive acting-out cause problems in elementary and secondary schools. ADD children who are not overactive often lack confidence and may develop only one or two best friends. Frequently on the fringe of their peer group, they often feel lonely and despondent.

Indications of poor peer relations are:

- Hits, bites, kicks and bosses other children
- Has difficulty following the rules of games and social interactions
- Is rejected or avoided by peers
- Is a loner and avoids group activities
- Teases peers and siblings excessively
- Bullies or bosses other children; wants to be the leader

Family Interaction Problems

Attention disorders have a profound effect on the family, especially if the child is hyperactive. The activity level, constant difficulties, moodiness, and problems at school create much tension and anxiety for the parents and siblings of these children. The support and assistance of a knowledgeable, caring teacher can be invaluable to a family struggling with the problems of attention disorders.

Indications of family interaction problems are:

- There is frequent family conflict.
- Activities and social gatherings are unpleasant.
- Parents argue over discipline since nothing works.
- Mother spends hours and hours on homework with ADHD child, leaving little time for others in family.
- Meals are frequently unpleasant.
- Arguments occur between parents and child over responsibilities and chores.
- Stress is continuous from child's social and academic problems.
- Parents, especially mother, feel:

__Frustrated   __Hopeless
__Alone   __Angry
__Guilty   __Afraid for child
__Helpless   __Disappointed
__Sad and
    depressed

Characteristics of ADHD/ADD
(Not in the *DSM-III-R*)

1. Extraordinary memory for remote events

2. Extraordinary attention to detail in drawing

3. Take it all in all at one time ("wide-angle lenses")

4. Marked fluctuation in performance

5. Difficulty internalizing the rules

6. Flight of ideas

7. Internally distracted, as well as externally

8. Require instant gratification

9. Overreact

10. Marked intensity

11. Poor organizational skills

12. Failure to anticipate consequences

13. Boredom

14. Brutally frank

15. Fatigue

16. Erratic sleeping habits (night terrors)

17. Kinesthetic learning is generally not affected

This chart appears in Stephen C. Copps, M.D., *The Attending Physician: Attention Deficit Disorder, A Guide for Pediatricians and Family Physicians.* Atlanta, Ga.: Southeastern Psychological Institute, 1992, 40. Reprinted by permission of the author.

Selected References on Attention Deficit Disorders

ADD Warehouse 1993 Catalog. Plantation, Fla.: ADD Warehouse, 1993.

This catalog, which is updated annually, contains specialized books, tapes, videos, assessment tools, texts, and games regarding attention deficit hyperactivity disorder. Materials are geared for a variety of individuals, including teachers, professors, assessment personnel, students, and parents. It is available from ADD Warehouse, 300 Northwest 70th Avenue, Suite 102, Plantation, FL 33317; telephone: 305-792-8944 or 1-800-233-9273.

Barkley, Russell A. *ADHD—What Can We Do?* New York: Guilford Publications, Inc., 1992. Video.

This 37-minute video presents a review of knowledge about the most useful approaches to managing attention deficit hyperactivity disorder (ADHD).

Barkley, Russell A. *ADHD—What Do We Know?* New York: Guilford Publications, Inc., 1992. Video.

This 37-minute video presents an informative review of current knowledge about ADHD.

Barkley, Russell A. *Attention Deficit Hyperactivity Disorder: A Handbook for Diagnosis and Treatment.* New York: The Guilford Press, 1990.

This comprehensive handbook for both practitioners and scientists provides analysis on the history of ADHD, primary symptoms, theories of its nature, associated conditions and etiologies, developmental course and outcome, and family context. Titles of topics covered within this comprehensive text are "Nature and Diagnosis," "Assessments," "Treatment" (including educational placement and classroom management), "Social Skills and Peer Relationship Training," "Medication Therapy," and "Assessment and Treatment of Adults with ADHD." The publications by Russell A. Barkley on ADHD cited in this list are available from the Guilford Press, 72 Spring Street, New York, NY 10012.

Fowler, Mary, and others. *CHADD Educators Manual: An In-depth Look at Attention Deficit Disorders from an Educational Perspective.* Fairfax, Va.: CASET Associates, 1993.

This book contains current information to assist all educators in educational manifestations, protocols for identification and assessment, principles and practices, of interventions, and problem-solving approaches. (CHADD is the acronym for Children with Attention Deficit Disorders.) This publication is available from CASET Associates, 3927 Old Lee Highway, Fairfax, VA 22030; telephone 1-800-545-5583.

---◆---

McCarney, Stephen B. *The Attention Deficit Disorders Intervention Manual.* Columbia, Mo.: Hawthorne Educational Services, Inc., 1990.

The school version of this manual provides classroom intervention strategies for the most common characteristics of attention deficit disorders exhibited by students in school situations. Strategies are designed as samples to assist professionals and teams in development of goals and objectives for individualized education programs (IEPs) as well as providing appropriate strategies in regular and special education classrooms. This publication is available from Hawthorne Educational Services, Inc., 800 Gray Oak Drive, Columbia, MO 65201; telephone (314) 874-1710.

Rief, Sandra F. *How to Reach and Teach ADD/ADHD Children: Practical Techniques and Strategies for Grades K–8.* Des Moines, Ia.: Center for Applied Research in Education, 1993.

This publication provides classroom-tested strategies, techniques, and interventions to help children with ADD/ADHD. It is written for educators, counselors, school nurses, psychologists, administrators, and parents. It focuses on the "whole child" and the team approach that enables professionals to guide these children toward academic and personal success. This publication is available from the Ordering Processing Department, Center for Applied Research in Education, P.O. Box 11071, Des Moines, IA 50336.

Glossary

Advocate. An individual, parent, or professional who promotes the interests of persons with disabilities.

Americans with Disabilities Act (ADA). The Americans with Disabilities Act of 1990 (P.L. 101–336) extends civil rights protection to people with disabilities. Effective dates are from 1990 through 1997. The legislation covers employment, public accommodations, transportation, state and local government operations, and telecommunications.

Appropriate education. A standard, required by law, to guarantee that students with disabilities receive an educational program individually tailored to their abilities and needs.

Assistive technology. Any item, piece of equipment, or product system (whether acquired commercially off the shelf, modified, or customized) that is used to increase, maintain, or improve functional capabilities of individuals with disabilities.

At-risk students. Students whose history (family, developmental, and medical), physical characteristics, life circumstances, or environment suggest that without intervention they will experience problems after graduation from school and during employment. This term also applies to a category of preschoolers under the age of three who are suspected of having a disability and are eligible for special services.

Attention deficit disorder or attention deficit hyperactivity disorder (ADD or ADHD). Developmentally inappropriate inattention and impulsivity. A disturbance lasting at least six months during which time at least eight of the following behaviors are present:

1. Often fidgets with hands or feet or squirms in seat (in adolescence may be limited to subjective feelings of restlessness)
2. Has difficulty in remaining seated when required to
3. Is easily distracted by extraneous stimuli
4. Has difficulty in awaiting turns in games or group situations
5. Often blurts out answers to questions before they have been completed
6. Has difficulty in following through on instructions from others (This behavior does not result from oppositional behavior or failure of comprehension.)
7. Has difficulty in sustaining attention in tasks or play activities
8. Often shifts from one uncompleted activity to another
9. Has difficulty in playing quietly
10. Often talks excessively
11. Often interrupts or intrudes on others
12. Often does not seem to listen to what is being said
13. Often loses things necessary for tasks or activities at school or at home
14. Often engages in physically dangerous activities without considering possible consequences (not for the purpose of thrill-seeking); for example, a child running into the street without looking[1]

---

[1]Adapted from the *Diagnostic and Statistical Manual of Mental Disorders DSM-III-R* (Third edition, revised). Washington, D.C.: American Psychiatric Association, 1987, pp. 52–53. Used by permission of the publisher.

Auditory perception. Ability to decode or encode auditory stimuli.

Behavioral goals and objectives. Expected and desired learning outcomes for students. The outcomes are stated in measurable terms so that the teaching and learning processes can be evaluated.

California Code of Regulations (CCR). The regulations authorized by *Education Code* sections, developed by the Department of Education, and approved by the State Board of Education and the Office of Administrative Law to provide standards and procedures for carrying out the provisions in the *Education Code.*

Categorical program. Services that are provided by special funding and are available only to a specific group of students; for example, low-income, underachieving, gifted, disabled, limited-English proficient, or migrant.

Code of Federal Regulations (CFR). Regulations developed by federal agencies to carry out the provisions of public laws. Most special education regulations are found in Section 34 of the *CFR.*

Collaboration. Group effort of special education teachers, regular education teachers, other service providers, and families working together to provide effective services and education.

Consulting teacher. A specially trained teacher who serves as a resource person to advise and provide instructional support to general education teachers whose students have disabilities.

Core curriculum. The basic academic subjects that are to be taught to all students.

Discrepancy formula. Formula required by the state to determine the "significant" difference between a student's actual achievement and expected achievement on the basis of scores of achievement and ability.

Discrepancy scores. The scores resulting from the application of a discrepancy formula used to determine eligibility for programs designed for students with learning disabilities.

Dyslexia. A disorder manifested by failure to attain the language skills of reading, writing, and spelling despite conventional instruction, adequate intelligence, and sociocultural opportunity.

Education Code. The laws passed by the California State Legislature pertaining to schools, libraries, and universities.

Free appropriate public education (FAPE). A major standard set forth in the Individuals with Disabilities Education Act (IDEA), which states that students with disabilities are entitled to free special services as needed in order to meet their individual educational needs.

Goals. See *Behavioral goals and objectives.*

High risk. See *At-risk.*

Hyperactivity. Has difficulty staying seated and sitting still and runs or climbs on things excessively.

Impulsivity. Acts before thinking, has difficulty taking turns, has problems organizing work, and shifts constantly from one activity to another.

Inattention. Fails to finish task started, is easily distractible, has a seeming lack of attention, and has difficulty concentrating on tasks requiring sustained attention.

Inclusion and full inclusion. An educational program in which students with disabilities remain in the classroom where they receive their specialized instruction and services.

Individualized education program (IEP). A written plan of instruction required by the Individuals with Disabilities Education Act (IDEA) for every school-age individual receiving special education. The plan must include a statement of the individual's strengths and weaknesses, long-term and short-term goals and objectives, and all special services required.

Individualized education program (IEP) team. Members of the team include all of the following: a representative designated by the school administration, the student's present teacher, a professional familiar with any assessment information, and one or both of the student's parents or a representative selected by the parent. When appropriate, the team also includes the student with exceptional needs, the special education teacher, and other individuals with the expertise or knowledge necessary for the development of the IEP.

Individualized instruction. Instruction planned to meet the individual needs of students through which they are provided with instructional tasks reflecting their own pace and style of learning.

Individuals with Disabilities Education Act (IDEA). Formerly referred to as the Education for All Handicapped Students Act (EHA). IDEA originally passed as PL 94-142 in 1975 and was amended in 1986 by PL 99-457, which provided for instruction and services for infants and toddlers. It was amended and reauthorized again in 1990 under PL 101-476, which strengthened transitional programs for adolescents and young adults with disabilities. IDEA ensures a free appropriate public education in the least restrictive environment for all students and youth with disabilities.

Instructional goals. A statement about learning that includes a result to be achieved after specific instruction. For example: The learner will increase his or her reading achievement by one grade level by the end of the school year.

Instructional objectives. Statements about learning that relate to an overall goal. Included are a description of the student's behavior, the conditions under which the behavior is to occur, and the criteria for acceptable performance.

Intellectual functioning. The actual performance of tasks believed to represent intelligence, such as observing, problem solving, and communicating.

Intelligence quotient (IQ). The numerical figure, with a score of 100 usually being average, obtained from a standardized test; often used to express mental development or ability.

Learning differences. Receiving instruction or demonstrating performance in ways that are not common for other students of the same age.

Learning difficulty. A student encounters problems in achieving school success, usually because of the manner in which instruction is presented or because of the demands made on performance when a learning difference is involved.

Learning disability. A disabling condition in which an individual with average intelligence is substantially delayed in academic achievement because of a processing disorder, not from an environmental, an economic, or a cultural disadvantage.

Learning strategies. Instructional methods to help students attend, listen, read, comprehend, and study more effectively by helping them organize and collect information systematically.

Least restrictive environment. A major principle of the IDEA which states that students with disabilities should be integrated and receive their education in the most normal setting with their age-related peers.

Limited-English proficiency. Limited ability to comprehend, read, write, or speak English.

Local educational agency (LEA). Typically, a local school district but may be a cooperative group of districts or counties that are funded as a single unit.

Mainstreaming. Keeping students who receive special education services in regular educational settings for some or all of their school day.

Other health impaired. A category of IDEA students who have limited strength, vitality, or alertness because of health problems.

Program specialist. A school district employee with expert knowledge about categorical programs and program options for students with disabilities.

Pullout activities. Students receive direct instruction, individually or in a small group, for part of the school day in a special setting away from the regular education classroom.

Resource specialist. A teacher who has received training in both regular and special education and who works with students with disabilities who need special education services for part of the school day.

School psychologist. A specialist who has received advanced training in developmental, cognitive, perceptual, and social and emotional functioning of children in a school setting.

Special classes. Classes used exclusively for students with special needs who need intensive, specialized instruction for more than half of the school day. Students are mainstreamed for part of the day if the IEP team feels that doing so is appropriate.

Special Education Local Plan Area (SELPA). A district or region that coordinates special education services for students residing in that attendance area.

Student study team (SST). A function of general education at a school site, with many differing names, used by a school faculty to bring staff together to discuss a student's problems and to explore ways the teacher or school can bring about improvement. The parent is often included on the team.

Time lines. When legal time limits are being calculated during the period between planning for referral and assessment and during the assessment process, calendar days are used, exclusive of time between terms and sessions.

Visual motor skill. Left/right clarity or confusion; fine motor, involving hand muscles; coordination necessary for writing skills; and gross motor, involving large-muscle control for running, kicking, throwing, and maneuvering the body.

Visual perception. Ability to decode and encode visual stimuli.

Selected References for General Information

Adelman, Howard S., and Linda Taylor. "The Problems of Definition and Differentiation and the Need for a Classification Schema," *Journal of Learning Disabilities,* Vol. 19, No. 9 (November, 1986), 514–20.

Baca, Leonard, and Phillip C. Chinn. "Coming to Grips with Cultural Diversity," *Exceptional Education Quarterly,* Vol. 2, No. 4 (February, 1982), 33–45.

Berk, Ronald A. *Screening and Diagnosis of Children with Learning Disabilities.* Springfield, Ill.: Charles C. Thomas, 1984. (Out of print)

California Special Education Programs: A Composite of Laws (Sixteenth edition). Sacramento: California Department of Education, 1994.

Compton, Carolyn. *A Guide to Eighty-five Tests for Special Education.* Belmont, Calif.: Fearon Book Publishing, 1990.

Copeland, Edna D., and Valerie L. Love. *Attention Without Tension: A Teacher's Handbook on Attention Disorders (ADHD and ADD)* (Revised edition). Atlanta, Ga.: Resurgens Press, Inc., 1992.

Copps, M.D., Stephen C. *The Attending Physician: Attention Deficit Disorder, A Guide for Pediatricians and Family Physicians.* Atlanta, Ga.: Southeastern Psychological Institute, 1992.

Diagnostic and Statistical Manual of Mental Disorders DSM-III-R (Third revised edition). Washington, D.C.: American Psychiatric Association, 1987.

Dinero, Thomas E.; Carol H. Donah; and Gerald L. Larson. "The Slingerland Screening Tests for Identifying Children with Specific Language Disability: Screening for Learning Disabilities in First Grade," *Perceptual and Motor Skills,* Vol. 49 (December, 1979), 971–78.

Eiserman, William D. "Three Types of Peer Tutoring: Effects on the Attitudes of Students with Learning Disabilities and Their Regular Class Peers," *Journal of Learning Disabilities*, Vol. 21, No. 4 (April, 1988), 249–52.

Fulmer, Susanne, and Robert Fulmer. "The Slingerland Tests: Reliability and Validity," *Journal of Learning Disabilities,* Vol. 16, No. 10 (December, 1983), 591–95.

Hambleton, R. K. "Advances in Criterion-referenced Testing Technology," in *The Handbook of School Psychology.* Edited by Terry B. Gutkin and Cecil R. Reynolds. New York: John Wiley and Sons, Inc., 1982.

Henry, Marcia R. "Beyond Phonics: Integrated Decoding and Spelling Instruction Based on Word Origin and Structure," *Annals of Dyslexia,* Vol. 38 (1988), 258–75.

Langdon, Henrette W. *Hispanic Children and Adults with Communication Disorders: Assessment and Intervention.* Gaithersburg, Md.: Aspen Publishers, Inc., 1992.

The Learning Disability Intervention Manual (Revised edition). Introduction by Stephen B. McCarney. Columbia, Mo.: Hawthorne Educational Services, 1989.

Lerner, Janet W. *Learning Disabilities: Theories, Diagnosis, and Teaching Strategies* (Fifth edition). Boston: Houghton Mifflin Company, 1988.

Levine, Melvin D. "Attention Deficits: The Diverse Affects of Weak Control Systems in Childhood," *Pediatric Annals*, Vol. 16, No. 2 (February, 1987), 117–30.

Levine, Melvin D. *Developmental Variation and Learning Disorders.* Cambridge, Mass.: Educators Publishing Service, Inc., 1987.

Levine, Melvin D. *Keeping Ahead in School.* Cambridge, Mass.: Educators Publishing Service, Inc., 1990.

Lovitt, Thomas C., and Dolores Michele DeMier. "An Evaluation of the Slingerland Method with LD Youngsters," *Journal of Learning Disabilities,* Vol. 17, No. 5 (May, 1984), 267–72.

McBurnett Keith; Benjamin Lahey; and Linda J. Piffner. "Diagnosis of Attention Deficit Disorders in DSM-IV: Scientific Basis and Implications for Education," *Exceptional Children,* Vol. 60, No. 2 (October/November, 1993), 108–17.

McCarney, Stephen B. *The Attention Deficit Disorders Intervention Manual.* Columbia, Mo.: Hawthorne Educational Services, 1990.

McCarney, Stephen B., and Kathy K. Cummins. *The Pre-Referral Intervention Manual.* Columbia, Mo.: Hawthorne Educational Services, 1988.

Meltzer, Lynn, and Bethany Solomon. *Educational Prescriptions for the Classroom for Students with Learning Problems.* Cambridge, Mass.: Educators Publishing Service, 1988.

Meyers, Marcee J. "Information Processing and the Slingerland Screening Tests," *Journal of Learning Disabilities*, Vol. 16, No. 3 (March, 1983), 150–53.

Program Guidelines for Language, Speech, and Hearing Specialists Providing Designated Instruction and Services. Sacramento: California Department of Education, 1990.

Reschly, D. J. "Nonbiased Assessment," in *School Psychology: Perspectives and Issues.* Edited by G. D. Phye and D. J. Reschly. New York: Academic Press, 1979.

Salvia, John, and James E. Ysseldyke. *Assessment in Special and Remedial Education* (Fifth edition). Boston: Houghton Mifflin Company, 1991.

Sattler, Jerome M. *Assessment of Children's Intelligence and Special Abilities* (Second edition). Boston: Allyn & Bacon, Inc., 1981.

Schools and the Culturally Diverse Exceptional Student: Promising Practices and Future Directions. Edited by Bruce Ramirez and Alba A. Ortiz. Reston, Va.: Council for Exceptional Children, 1988.

Sheffield, Betty. "The Structured Flexibility of Orton-Gillingham," *Annals of Dyslexia,* Vol. 41 (1991), 41–54.

Smith, Jill, and Howard Diller. *Learning Disabilities: What to Do After Diagnosis.* In four volumes. Dallas: Apodoxis Press, 1991. (Vol. 1: *A Survival Guide, Kindergarten Through Third Grade,* 1991; Vol. 2: *A Survival Guide, Fourth Through Sixth Grade,* 1991; Vol 3: *A Survival Guide, Seventh Through Twelfth Grade,* 1991; Vol. 4: *A Survival Guide, College and the Workplace,* 1992.)

Special Education Rights and Responsibilities. San Francisco: Community Alliance for Special Education and Protection and Advocacy, 1994.

Tarnopol, Lester. "Introduction to Children with Learning Disabilities," in *Learning Disabilities: Introduction to Educational and Medical Management.* Springfield, Ill.: Charles C. Thomas, 1969.

Wallace, Gerald; Stephen C. Larsen; and L. K. Elksnin. *Educational Assessment of Learning Problems: Testing for Teaching* (Second edition). Boston: Allyn & Bacon, Inc., 1992.

Zentall, Sydney S. "Research on the Educational Implications of Attention Deficit Hyperactivity Disorder," *Exceptional Children,* Vol. 60, No. 2 (October/November, 1993), 143–53.

Zigmond, Naomi, and others. *Teaching Learning Disabled Students at the Secondary School Level.* Reston, Va.: Council for Exceptional Children, 1985. ERIC, ED 268702.